Norwegian Pick-up Bandweaving

Heather Torgenrud

Schiffer Publishing Ltd

4880 Lower Valley Road • Atglen, PA 19310

Published by Schiffer Publishing, Ltd.
4880 Lower Valley Road
Atglen, PA 19310
Phone: (610) 593-1777; Fax: (610) 593-2002
E-mail: Info@schifferbooks.com

For our complete selection of fine books on this and related subjects, please visit our website at www.schifferbooks.com. You may also write for a free catalog.

This book may be purchased from the publisher. Please try your bookstore first.

We are always looking for people to write books on new and related subjects. If you have an idea for a book, please contact us at proposals@schifferbooks.com

Schiffer Publishing's titles are available at special discounts for bulk purchases for sales promotions or premiums. Special editions, including personalized covers, corporate imprints, and excerpts can be created in large quantities for special needs. For more information, contact the publisher.

Credits for images

Photographs from Vesterheim by Alison Dwyer, Vesterheim Norwegian-American Museum.

Photographs in Part 3 by Marti de Alva, River Song Photography.

All other photographs from sources noted in captions.

Diagrams, drawings, and charts by Author.

On the Cover: Image ©2014 Artists Rights Society (ARS), New York/KUVASTO, Helsinki. Juho Rissanen, *Nauhankutoja* (Ribbon Weaver), 1908. Ostrobothnian Museum. Photo: Erkki Salminen. Artist Juho Rissanen (1873–1950) was born in a rural area of Finland and grew up in poverty. He considered himself an illustrator of people and often depicted ordinary Finns at work. Although the ribbon weaver in the painting was Finnish (Eriikka Lipponen from Nilsiä), her weaving method was the same as that used in Norway. Patterned bands or ribbons made in this way were used in folk costumes and wedding celebrations in Finland and Sweden as well as in Norway.

Copyright © 2014 by Heather Torgenrud

Library of Congress Control Number: 2014950995

Cover design by RoS
Designed by Heather Torgenrud

Type set in Myriad Pro/Adobe Garamond Pro

ISBN: 978-0-7643-4751-1
Printed in China

Other Schiffer Books on Related Subjects:

Hex Weave & Mad Weave: An Introduction to Triaxial Weaving.
Elizabeth Harris and Charlene St. John
978-0-7643-4465-7. $24.99

Universal Stitches for Weaving, Embroidery, and Other Fiber Arts.
Nancy Arthur Hoskins
978-0-7643-4431-2. $24.99

Tapestry Handbook: The Next Generation.
Carol Russell
978-0-7643-2756-8. $59.95

Dedication

In loving memory of my husband, Don Torgenrud (1942–2008),
who gave me the loom, led me to study Norwegian,
and supported me in everything.

Norwegian Counties

Finnmark

Troms

Nordland

Nord-Trøndelag

Trondheim
Trøndelag

Sør-Trøndelag

Møre og Romsdal

Røros

Nord-Østerdalen

Nordfjord

Gudbrandsdalen

Hedmark

Sogn og Fjordane

Sunnfjord

Oppland

Østerdalen

Valdres

Lillehammer

Hordaland

Bergen

Hallingdal

Hadeland

Buskerud

Hardanger

Numedal

Romerike

Oslo

Vest-Telemark

Rogaland

Telemark

Akershus

Setesdal

Øst-Telemark

Østfold

Vestfold

Stavanger

Aust-Agder

Agder

Vest-Agder

Kristiansand

Borders for map: Kartverket

Historical Regions

Bandweaving traditions are rooted in the historical regions of Norway, which were often defined by geographical elements like river valleys and fjords. Regions mentioned in the book and shown in green on the map are:

Agder area in southern Norway
Gudbrandsdalen river valley in Oppland
Hadeland area in Oppland
Hallingdal river valley in Buskerud
Hardanger fjord area in Hordaland
Nordfjord fjord area in Sogn og Fjordane
Nord-Østerdalen north part of Østerdalen
Numedal river valley in Buskerud
Romerike area in Akershus
Setesdal river valley in Aust-Agder
Sunnfjord fjord area in Sogn og Fjordane
Trøndelag area in central Norway
Valdres river valley in Oppland
Vest-Telemark western part of Telemark
Østerdalen river valley in Hedmark
Øst-Telemark eastern part of Telemark

Contents

Fig. 1: Pick-up-woven bands spilling out of wooden trunk,
collection of Vesterheim Norwegian-American Museum.
Photo: Alison Dwyer/Vesterheim.

Acknowledgments

I'm deeply grateful to many people for their help and encouragement, especially to:

Laurann Gilbertson, Chief Curator of Vesterheim Norwegian-American Museum, for generous help with research from the beginning.

Jean Scorgie, of Weaver's Craft, and Mary Skoy, of the Norwegian Textile Guild, for reviewing the manuscript and giving thoughtful editing help.

Kristine Sødal, my language teacher, and her mother-in-law, Kirsten Sødal, of Kristiansand, Norway, for their friendship and help with Norwegian.

Anne Grete Stuksrud, and her assistant, Ragnhild Wold, of Lillehammer, Norway, for their teaching expertise and enthusiasm for the craft.

Helga Reidun Bergebakken Nesset, of Nordøsterdalsmuseet, for her kind assistance.

Inger Lise Christie, of Oslo, Norway, for sending her booklet on tablet weaving, which contained important information on the history of pick-up.

Alison Dwyer, of Vesterheim Norwegian-American Museum, for the photos in **Part 2**.

Marti de Alva, of River Song Photography, for the photos in **Part 3**.

Joanne Hall, of Glimåkra USA, for warping and weaving supplies.

Susan Wilson, Sara Lamb, Abby Franquemont, and Kathleen Stokker, for advice and encouragement.

Ingebjørg Monsen, Kay Larson, Mary Skoy, Susan Kolstad-Onken, Jan Mostrom, Solveig Pollei, Veronna Caponne, Lisa Ellis, and the other weavers on the 2007 Vesterheim Textile Tour to Norway and Sweden.

Dan Rude, Betty Wing, Hayden Ausland, and Normanden 424, the local Sons of Norway lodge in Missoula, Montana, where most of the photos in **Part 3** were taken.

The Sons of Norway Foundation, for a 2007 General Heritage & Culture Grant to help with research expenses.

My fellow weavers in the Missoula Weavers' Guild.

My friend, Lorraine Shook, for pitching in as Girl Friday whenever needed.

My mother, Margaret Carson, whose love of books and writing was an inspiration.

And finally, I'd like to thank my editor, Tina Libby, and the folks at Schiffer, without whom this book would not be possible.

Introduction

In 1996, Queen Sonja of Norway presided over the opening of a new folk museum building in the little mountain community of Tynset. But it was no ordinary ribbon-cutting ceremony. Instead, two red and white pick-up bands tied across the main doorway were untied with a flourish.[1] It was fitting symbolism, since the museum's collection of bands represents a craft that has been an important part of Norwegian folk culture for hundreds of years.

It's easy to see why pick-up weaving has endured for so long. Just look at the bands spilling out of the little wooden trunk in Fig. 1 and see if you find, as I do, that pick-up bands with their vivid colors, pleasing motifs, and interesting texture are as beautiful as any textile in the world, large or small.

Discovering a living tradition

I've been intrigued by pick-up weaving for years, ever since the early 1970s when I was still in my teens and learning to weave. My husband-to-be gave me an inkle loom as a gift and pick-up quickly became my favorite technique. I was fascinated with working out patterns on graph paper and with the rhythmic way the patterns took shape in my hands.

Back then, I didn't know anything about Norwegian bandweaving traditions. The book I learned from, *Byways in Handweaving* by Mary Meigs Atwater, told me that my shuttle was a "Norwegian belt shuttle," that my favorite threading was the one "used in Europe," and that a loom similar to my inkle loom was "shown in Scandinavian books on weaving."[2] Beyond that, information was scarce. I taught many classes in pick-up over the years and wrote an article for *Handwoven* magazine in 1996, always wishing I knew more about the history of this technique and how such bands were used in the old days.

Then, in the late 1990s, something unexpected happened. My husband and I were taking a Norwegian language class and our teacher wore her traditional Vest-Agder dress for a talk about the importance of regional costumes in modern Norway. Peeking out from beneath her rust-red bodice were suspenders woven in pick-up. Could it be that in Norway I would find not only the connection with history I had always longed for, but a living tradition as well?

Later, our teacher's mother-in-law visited Montana from Norway and saw the pick-up bands I'd woven. When I told her I was interested in the history of the technique, she sent me a small booklet on bandweaving from Norway that whetted my appetite for more.

Fig. 2: *Bandgrind* (band heddle) carved from one piece of birch.
Photo: Vesterheim (1979.80.2).

Fig. 3: *Bandgrind* (band heddle),
birch, chip-carved decoration.
Photo: Vesterheim (1980.67.2).

How this book came to be

I began my search for information at Vesterheim Norwegian-American Museum in Decorah, Iowa. Curator Laurann Gilbertson pointed me to a number of Norwegian-language books and articles in the Vesterheim library which, together with the museum's collection of bands, formed a solid base for my research. I'm especially grateful for this invaluable help.

In the years that followed, I collected many Norwegian books and embarked on an enjoyable treasure hunt. I did not find a Norwegian book that told the whole story of pick-up weaving, the one I had always longed to read. But because the cultural conditions in Norway allowed bandweaving to survive well into the 1800s and the country then worked to preserve its folk traditions, the threads of the story were there and I found them in dozens of places. Over time a fascinating picture emerged and I became passionate about putting it into book form.

I am indebted to four authors in particular whose works made it possible to tell this story: Inger Lise Christie has published several studies about swaddling bands, and pick-up was one of the techniques used to make them. Torbjørg Gauslaa documented a group of interesting cushion covers from Nord-Østerdalen sewn from pick-up bands. Aagot Noss has written extensively about folk dress, in which pick-up bands played a role. And Marta Hoffmann documented textile tools and looms, including those used for pick-up weaving.

In 2007, I traveled to Norway and Sweden on the Vesterheim Textile Tour led by Laurann Gilbertson and Ingebjørg Monsen, a Norwegian weaving teacher. Along with a group of fellow weavers, many from the Norwegian Textile Guild, I studied pick-up techniques with bandweaving expert Anne Grete Stuksrud in Lillehammer and saw a unique collection of bands at Nordøsterdalsmuseet in Tynset. Since comprehensive instructions for weaving pick-up on traditional hole-and-slot band heddles are not available in English, it seemed natural to include a how-to section in this book.

What this book is about

In **Part 1 History & Tradition**, we'll look at the customs surrounding bandweaving in rural Norway in the 1700s and 1800s. In **Part 2 Vesterheim Collection**, we'll look at some of the bands brought to this country by Norwegian immigrants. In **Part 3 How to Weave Pick-up**, there are complete, step-by-step instructions for weaving pick-up bands. **Parts 2** and **3** include charts for more than 100 traditional patterns.

This book is about pick-up bands. Other kinds of Norwegian bands—those made by tablet weaving, tapestry weaving, and finger weaving—are not included.

The focus is on bands from the rural valleys of eastern and southern Norway and the inner fjord regions of western Norway. Although the Sami people of northern Norway have a rich history of pick-up bandweaving, many of their traditions are different and are beyond the scope of this book.

What is Norwegian pick-up bandweaving?

Pick-up is a technique for weaving narrow bands or ribbons that are both decorative and practical. It begins with a threading in contrasting colors like red and white. Patterns are formed by picking up certain threads on each row. The distinctive patterns are an integral part of the fabric structure and can be endlessly varied. There are two traditional pick-up weaves in Norway, shown in Figs. 4 and 5. Each requires a different order of colors in the threading and produces different kinds of motifs.

The term "pick-up" can also be applied to techniques for weaving other kinds of textiles, but as used in this book it refers to techniques for weaving bands.

I've placed the technical information about the weaving processes, pick-up techniques, and weave structures in **Part 3**, so that readers who are not weavers can enjoy the rest of the book without having to learn the vocabulary of weaving. The one exception: in describing traditional band looms at the end of **Part 1** it was necessary to define and use some basic weaving terms.

A link to the past

Whether you are interested in reading about Norwegian folk art, textiles, or traditional customs, or whether you want to learn the weaving techniques themselves, this book will introduce you to a unique craft that has been known in Norway at least since the 1600s. Pick-up bands played an important role in many customs in the old Norwegian farm society—from the way a baby was swaddled or a young girl's hair was braided to the way a basket of food was tied up for a neighbor's wedding celebration.

This story, which unfolds in **Part 1**, gives us a unique window into that society and, like the process of pick-up weaving itself, offers a deeply satisfying connection with the past.

Fig. 4: *Stuttband* (band used in the old days to hold up outer skirt to keep it clean) from Nord-Østerdalen in one of the two traditional Norwegian pick-up weaves. Museumssentret Ramsmoen, Tynset, Norway, 2007.
Photo: Author.

Fig. 5: Suspenders from Nord-Østerdalen in one of the two traditional Norwegian pick-up weaves. Museumssentret Ramsmoen, Tynset, Norway, 2007.
Photo: Author.

Part 1
History & Tradition

Pick-up weaving is a technique for making beautifully-patterned bands. The distinctive motifs are an integral part of the weave structure and appear embossed in vivid color on a textured background. The technique flourished for hundreds of years in the rural communities of Scandinavia, with different places developing unique styles of pattern and color.

Pick-up bands are both decorative and strong, well-suited for a variety of practical purposes. In Norway they were used for belts, apron bands, hairbands, stocking bands, suspenders, swaddling bands, carrying straps, and ties for baskets of food. Motifs like diagonal crosses or X-shapes, diamonds, hearts, and eight-petaled roses were typically woven in red wool on a light-colored background of linen or cotton, with other colors used for accents and borders.

These striking bands were part of Norway's folk traditions in many districts from at least the late 1600s well into the 1800s. We'll look first at the culture and customs that surrounded pick-up weaving during those years and allowed it to survive to the present day. Then we'll look at bandweaving looms and the clues they provide about the history of the technique.

The Old Rural Society

Like the other folk arts and crafts, pick-up weaving was the product of an old rural society that had changed very little since the Middle Ages. At the heart of this society were the farms and the valleys in which they were located.

In 1800, nine out of ten Norwegians lived on farms. A typical farmstead had a central courtyard surrounded by a cluster of wood buildings, weathered and gray. One was a single-room dwelling with beds, table, and an open hearth. Another was a storehouse where grain, dried food, and church-going clothes were kept. Other buildings might include a loft with beds for the hired help, a cookhouse, a shed for firewood and tools, a hay barn, and barns for the pigs, sheep, cows, and horse. Away from the courtyard there was often a smithy, and beyond that a smaller dwelling for the cotter (tenant farmer) and his family who lived on the farm in exchange for labor. All around was a patchwork of fields and meadows with narrow roads leading to neighboring farms and the parish church.

These neighboring farms formed a community, but there were no shops in the country districts prior to the mid-1800s. Before that, laws protected merchants in towns and prohibited markets except at prescribed locations at certain times of the year. Farm families tried to be as self-sufficient as possible, but there were always some things they needed to get from the market or from a local craftsman.

Fig. 6: Torbjørg Fidjeland with baby in pick-up band sling, bucket, and rake, Vest-Agder, 1936. *Photo: Anna Grostøl/Norsk Folkemuseum.*

Fig. 7: Storehouse in farm courtyard,
Telemark, 1860s or 1870s.
Photo: Henry Rosling/Norsk Folkemuseum.

The traditional districts of the country were defined by the landscape, with settlements centered in large river valleys and around fjords and separated by mountain ranges. Each district naturally developed its own identity— in dialect, style of dress, and folk art—while still remaining distinctly Norwegian.

Farm families worked at logging, hunting, and fishing to supplement farm production. They grew grain and vegetables, gathered berries, tended the animals, made butter and cheese, and put up hay for the winter. The work was strenuous and the work day was long for everyone in the family.

Skill with the hands was highly valued. While both men and women did farm work, crafts were divided traditionally, with women doing the spinning, weaving, knitting, and sewing and men doing the carpentry, wood carving, leatherwork, and metalwork. In the wintertime, in the light from the fireplace, whale oil lamp, or tallow candles, men repaired tools and made containers and furniture, while women spun yarn and wove cloth the family would need in the coming year.

Sundays and important occasions meant a break from work and were something to look forward to. For church feast days, such as Christmas, Easter, and Pentecost, families prepared special foods and wore their best clothes.

Rural culture was deeply rooted in tradition. And as we'll see, pick-up bands were used in many time-honored customs, from wedding celebrations to christenings. Despite the hardships of daily life, farm women took time to create items of great beauty, to weave bands in intricate pick-up patterns instead of simpler and more utilitarian plain weave—an indication that the bands had a greater significance beyond their practical use.

Fig. 8: Woman carrying porridge container wrapped with pick-up band, Telemark, 1909.
Photo: Johan J. Meyer/Norsk Folkemuseum.

Textile Traditions

In the old days a young girl's education in the textile arts began early. To have good prospects for marriage she needed to be able to spin yarn and weave the cloth that would be needed to clothe her family and furnish her home. This included not just purely utilitarian fabrics but also decorative coverlets, special christening blankets, and beautifully-patterned bands.

From her mother and the other women living on the farm, she learned about the whole labor-intensive cycle of textile production. This included tending the sheep, shearing them, and cleaning, sorting, and carding the wool. If the family grew flax it would include harvesting the plants, then retting, breaking, scutching, and hackling to separate the linen fibers from the stems and prepare them for spinning.

Fig. 9: Adolph Tidemand (1814–1876), *Spinnersken* (The Spinner), 1857. *Photo©: O. Væring Eftf. AS.*

Fig. 11: Bandgrind with band knife, from Hallingdal in Buskerud. Small hole-and-slot heddles like this one were commonly used for pick-up bandweaving in Norway. *Photo: Anne-Lise Reinsfelt/Norsk Folkemuseum.*

Fig. 10: Image ©2014 Artists Rights Society (ARS), New York/KUVASTO, Helsinki. Juho Rissanen (1873–1950), *Nauhankutoja* (Ribbon Weaver), 1908. The weaver is Finnish, but her method of weaving on the hole-and-slot band heddle is the same as that used in Norway. *Photo: Erkki Salminen/Ostrobothnian Museum.*

She learned how to spin the fibers into yarn and how to dye the yarn with colors made from bark, roots, leaves, and lichens gathered from the countryside, as well as sewing and knitting. She learned how to weave on a band loom and on the large floor loom that was set up in the home each winter. She worked alongside the adult women from the time she was small, being given only the simplest tasks at first, like carding wool and skeining yarn, before learning to weave.

In anticipation of her wedding day, it was customary for a young woman to fill her bridal chest with textiles she had woven and sewn, such as clothing, coverlets, and tablecloths. This trousseau would be an important part of what she would bring into her marriage and it usually included baby clothes and swaddling bands. In Østerdalen the items for a baby would be kept in a wooden box called a *bånklælaup* (baby-clothes box).

A girl's ability to weave beautiful pick-up bands demonstrated her skill and artisanship and brought her the respect of others in the community. In some

Fig. 12: Bandgrind with carved initials AS LD and year 1827, Røros, Sør-Trøndelag. *Photo: Anne-Lise Reinsfelt/Norsk Folkemuseum.*

areas it was customary for a girl to weave pick-up bands to give as bridal gifts at her wedding, and these were highly prized by the recipients. In Setesdal, the bride and her mother made belts to give to the groom's mother and sisters. In Nord-Østerdalen, Torbjørg Gauslaa recorded the memories of Berit Vang Moen of Vingelen, who said, *"Mor gifte seg i 1898, og andre bryllaupsdagen hadde ho forkle-fanget fullt av rosa-votter og band til utdeling."* (Mother got married in 1898, and on the second day of the wedding she had an apron full of bands and rose-patterned mittens to pass out.)[3]

To keep up with all of her work a woman had to keep her hands busy and she picked up handwork whenever she sat down to rest. *Tida skulle nyttes* (time shall be made use of) was one saying. Often a woman even kept her hands busy as she walked from place to place, carrying knitting or a drop spindle. Bandweaving was a stationary activity done while sitting, but because the *bandgrind* (hole-and-slot heddle used for bandweaving, plural *bandgrinder*) was small and portable it could easily be brought along—when girls traveled to the mountain cottage to tend the sheep as they grazed in the high summer pastures, for example.

Gauslaa wrote that in Trysil in Østerdalen, people remembered that when Olea Gjermundsdatter Lyseggen (1825–1903) tended the cows in the woods she usually had her bandgrind with her.[4] One of the things Olea wove was a baby coverlet in pick-up, in white cotton and red wool. It was made by sewing together nineteen bands and trimming the edges with other bands in a lattice pattern. See Fig. 13.

Sometimes woven goods were not produced on the farm but obtained from local women who specialized in the craft. These professional weavers were often women with little income—widows, unmarried women, or wives or daughters on small farms or cotters' places. Although the work did not pay well, they wove for sale in order to support themselves and often developed a high level of skill.

One such woman was Hælge Olsdotter Innleggen (1840–1923), an unmarried cotter's daughter who settled at Innleggen farm in Sauherad in Øst-Telemark. She was called Hælge *Beltevever* (Belt-Weaver), and although she was best known for the superior quality of her tablet-woven sashes, she was an expert in many textile arts, including pick-up weaving. Her bands were highly sought after. It was said that every spring she traveled to market with several bags full of belts that she had woven during the winter and she also sold her work to a shop in Oslo. In 1998 the cottage where she had lived was restored and moved to the grounds at Evju Bygdetun museum in Sauherad. Among the items in the Sash Weaver's Cottage, as it is called, are a threaded bandgrind and a pick-up basket band.[5]

Fig. 13: Drawing of patterns from one corner of baby coverlet made by Olea Gjermundsdatter Lyseggen, of Trysil in Østerdalen, by sewing pick-up bands together.

In Setesdal, where bandgrinder were not known and larger looms were used to weave bands, bandweaving was often a specialty of the women who owned the looms. While a floor loom for weaving cloth was found on most farms, the Setesdal band loom and the knowledge required to weave pick-up bands was not as widespread. Often band looms and the related skills were passed down in a family from one generation to the next, and the bands these women made were often traded or sold to others.

Courting Gifts

Many of the bandgrinder preserved in museum collections are highly decorated with carved or painted designs, like hearts, birds, and flowers. This is because in the old farm society of the 1700s and 1800s these small textile tools were often used as *friergaver* (courting gifts).

According to Harald Kolstad, customs varied from district to district, but a relationship often began with a small handmade gift, sometimes presented by the young man's friend. If the young woman chose to keep the gift the courtship could continue, and if she did not like the suitor, the gift would be returned. As a relationship became more serious, the gifts became finer and these were sometimes purchased from a local craftsman.[6]

A common courting gift, the bandgrind was a practical item that a young woman could use in her daily work to weave apron bands, swaddling bands, and stocking bands. As a courting gift it also became a prized heirloom. Many were inscribed with her initials and the year, along with symbols like the cross for faith and the heart for love. It was said, *"Jo finere skåret, jo kjærere frier"* (The finer the carving, the dearer the suitor).[7]

Young women sometimes gave gifts in return. These were almost always textile items like knitted mittens or stockings, or suspenders or stocking

Fig. 14: Bandgrind, initials MJD and year 1864 painted on front.
Photo: Vesterheim (Luther College Collection 1403).

Fig. 15: Nils Bergslien (1853–1928), *Et frieri* (A Courting), undated.
Photo©: O. Væring Eftf. AS.

bands woven in pick-up in beautiful colors and patterns. In response to a questionnaire sent out by the *Norsk Etnologisk Gransking* (Norwegian Ethnological Study, a department of Norsk Folkemuseum) a response from Buskerud about courting customs said that *"hun kunne ha et par riktig forseggjorte sokkeband til han"* (she could have a pair of very nicely-made stocking bands for him).[8]

The handmade gifts that the young couple exchanged communicated more than the personal feelings that were difficult to put into words. They demonstrated skills and values that would be important for their future life together. The gift of a finely-carved bandgrind spoke to the young woman of her suitor's ability to make furniture and tools and the importance he placed on good workmanship. And her gift of woven stocking bands was a symbol of the skill and diligence she would bring to the necessary task of weaving household linens and clothing fabrics for the family.

Folk Dress

Bandweaving was preserved in the strong traditions of *folkedrakt* (folk dress) that continued in rural Norway into the mid- and late 1800s, and even into the mid-1900s in some areas.

The term "folk dress" refers to the clothing formerly worn by rural Norwegians. In many areas pick-up bands were used for part of the woman's costume, as *belter* (belts), *forkleband* (apron bands), *seler* (suspenders), *hårband* (hairbands), *strømpeband* (stocking bands), and *kante- og pynteband* (edging and decorative bands).

Dress for women usually included a headdress, jacket, skirt with separate or attached bodice, shirt, under-skirt, belt, apron, stockings, and shoes. The cut and style of decoration developed differently in different places, with each valley or region having its own characteristic costumes, distinct from those of neighboring regions.

Throughout a region the choice of colors and materials varied somewhat from person to person within the boundaries of accepted local customs, while the cut and style of decoration remained the same. Dress played a large role in reinforcing a sense of local identity and at the same time could signify the occupation, age, or marital status of the wearer.

In this excerpt from the Norwegian folk tale, *Berthe Tuppenhaugs fortellinger* (Berthe Tuppenhaug's Stories), bands are one way a woman's garment is identified as being from a specific place (Hadeland) and of a specific type (Sunday best): *"Hun var helligdagspyntet, det vil si, hun var iført den drakten som var brukelig blant gamle folk i hennes hjembygd Hadeland, hun var kommet over til Romerike derfra: en blå trøye, kantet med vevede bånd, sort foldet stakk, lue med skruv og nakketufse."* (She was in her Sunday best, that is to say she was wearing the costume that was common among older folks in her native district of Hadeland, from whence she had come to Romerike: a blue jacket, edged with woven bands, black pleated skirt, and high-stuffed cap with laced brim and neck fringe.)[9]

Fig. 16: Adolph Tidemand (1814–1876), untitled portrait of Aslaug Bjørnsdatter Mosebøe, of Sauland in Øst-Telemark, 1844. She is wearing a pick-up apron band with tabs and tassels at the ends. *Photo©: O. Væring Eftf. AS.*

For both social and economic reasons, folk costumes changed very slowly. But they did evolve naturally over time, retaining their local identities while incorporating new techniques and fashion elements from elsewhere in Europe. Not all of the fabric in folk costumes was handwoven. Imported cloth and ribbons were sometimes used for finer pieces.

Dress for everyday use was plain, without trim or ornamentation. It was often skillfully mended, displaying the important values of thrift and handiness. In Setesdal, where a pick-up belt was worn with the church-going clothes, a belt in plain weave would be worn over an everyday dress.

For church wear a separate costume was worn. It could be cut the same as the everyday costume but was often of finer material and highly decorated, and it could be further adorned for special celebrations. A church-going costume that was old and worn could be converted to everyday use by removing the trim. Nothing was thrown away if it could still be used.

Pick-up bands were also used as *stuttband* (shortening bands), which were needed in the old days since handwoven skirts were long and heavy. When a woman needed to keep her skirt clean, on the way to church or while she was working, she held the outer skirt part way up with a band and let the under-skirt show a little. The band shown in Fig. 4 is a shortening band.

Folk dress was an integral part of the rural society, governed by time-honored local customs passed down from one generation to the next. And with those customs came a heritage of knowledge and skills in the textile arts that in many districts included pick-up weaving.

The use of pick-up bands in folk dress can be traced back to the late 1600s. In researching Vest-Telemark customs, where pick-up bands are used for hairbands and apron bands, Aagot Noss looked at probate records from the late 1600s to the early 1800s. She found a number of bands listed in the inventories, the oldest being from 1697 in Vinje. Many were identified as *kringlet* bands and belts, a word that describes the diamond-like motif common in pick-up. Some *kringlet* bands were further identified as *7-kringlet* (from 1697 in Vinje), *5-kringlet* (from 1709 in Kviteseid), *3-kringlet* (from 1767 and 1774 in Kviteseid) and *full-kringlet* (from 1741 in Lårdal). She also found other entries for bands from the same period that referred to the *kross* (cross or diagonal cross) and *krok* (crooked line or zigzag) motifs common in pick-up.[10]

In Setesdal, where pick-up weaving is used for hairbands and belts, the technique has also been established for hundreds of years. According to Noss, in Setesdal the folk dress has "been the same as far back as documentation goes," from the 1600s to the 1900s (except for a head scarf worn by both married and unmarried women that came into use in the early 1800s).[11]

Hairbands

In many districts in the old days, narrow woven *hårband* (hairbands) were used by both girls and married women to braid their hair. Pick-up weaving was commonly used for hairbands in Vest-Telemark, Tinn in upper Telemark, Setesdal and upper Hallingdal, among other places. In Øst-Telemark, tablet-woven hairbands became very common, but many photographs from that area in the 1800s show pick-up bands instead.

The hair was divided into two pigtails on each side of a center part. The center of the band was placed at the back of the neck and half of the band was used to wrap each pigtail. One saying held that when a girl was ready to begin wrapping she could make a wish. If the bands on either side of the head were the same length when she was done, the wish would come true.

Fig. 17: Woman's headdress for church wear, pick-up hairband, from Hallingdal in Buskerud.
Photo: Norsk Folkemuseum.

In Tinn, Vest-Telemark, and Setesdal, each pigtail was divided into two sections and the band was wrapped around first one and then the other section in a figure-eight pattern with the hair visible between the turns of the band. The plaits hung down in back under a head scarf, but when girls were bare-headed the plaits were laid around the crown of the head in a wreath shape with the ends of the band knotted together at the back of the neck. In upper Hallingdal, upper Valdres, and Sogn, the band was wrapped so closely that the hair was completely hidden.

The length of a hairband varied depending on the wrapping method and the length of the hair. In Vest-Telemark hairbands were usually about ½" wide and about 90" long.

Fig. 18: Adolph Tidemand (1814–1876), Portrait of Gunild Olsdatter from Tinn, 1848. Her hair is plaited with a band and coiled around her head.
Photo: Anne Hansteen Jarre/Nasjonalmuseet for kunst, arkitektur og design/The National Museum of Art, Architecture and Design.

In 1782, a writer described the custom in Tinn: *"Pigerne har deres Haar flettet i 2de Dele, eller Fletninger, hvori er flettet et bred spraglet Baand, og fæstet omkring Hovedet."* (The girls have their hair plaited in two parts or braids, in which is plaited a wide, multi-colored band, and fastened around the head.)[12]

These plaits were used beginning at age three or four or as soon as the hair was shoulder length. Gunhild Lyngtveit of Bykle, Setesdal, who was born in 1902, told Aagot Noss in 1966 that girls who had short hair could wrap the hairband around the head without braiding and let the ends hang down in back.[13]

In upper Hallingdal, hairbands were commonly about four yards long and the hair was coiled differently than in Telemark and Setesdal. A special coil was used as a base for the traditional headdresses—the *jentepannelin* (girl's linen head scarf) for young girls, the *huvuklut* (head cloth) for older girls, and the *hettebunad* (headdress) for married women.

According to Noss, hairbands and headdresses were used in Hallingdal at least from the last half of the 1600s up until the 1870s or 1880s. In the old days a wife would wear a headdress every day, with different coverings and accessories for special occasions. Eventually the everyday headdress was discontinued.[14]

Men's Clothing

Pick-up bands were also used in men's folk dress, primarily for *sokkeband* or *strømpeband* (stocking bands) with knee-length breeches, *bukseseler* (suspenders), and *pelsband* (coat bands).

In Nord-Østerdalen, men wore *snøsokker* (footless snow socks or gaiters) to keep the snow from getting into the tops of their shoes. These were made of thick, fulled wool fabric called *vadmel*, with a wedge-shaped gusset over the instep and a split at the top of the calf. A narrow stirrup of leather was fastened around the bottom of the foot and the tops were held up with a band, called a *hussuband*, that could be woven in pick-up.

Puttis (puttees) were wrapped around the calf from ankle to knee, to keep out the cold and snow. They were often made from strips of wool cloth but pick-up bands could be used. Sometimes women wore puttees too.

In the days when horse-drawn sleds were the main mode of winter transportation, even up until the 1930s and 1940s in some areas, men wore long, fur driving coats with collars to keep out the bitter cold. These coats did not have buttons, so a band, often woven in pick-up, was used as a fastener to hold the coat closely around the neck and body for warmth. Such a coat was called either a *mudd* or *pels* (fur coat). In some areas "mudd" referred to an everyday driving coat made of sheepskin, while "pels" referred to a driving coat made of wolf, dog, reindeer, or bear pelts.

Fig. 19: Andreas Bloch (1860–1917), *Mann i pels, med pisk i hånden* (Man in Fur Coat, with Whip in Hand). His coat is fastened with a band.
Photo: Jeanette Veiby/Nasjonalmuseet for kunst, arkitektur og design/The National Museum of Art, Architecture and Design.

The fastening band was called a *muddband* or *pelsband* (coat band), and was usually about four yards long and a couple of inches wide. It was laid over the back of the neck, then the two sides were either twisted together in front, as shown in Fig. 19, or crossed over the chest before being taken to the back and tied around the waist. A big wolf-skin coat decorated with a colorful and intricately-patterned band made an impressive picture.

Swaddling Customs

Pick-up bands were preserved, not only in adult folk dress, but in the tradition of *reiving* (swaddling) babies. This ancient custom was once widespread in all of Europe and much of the rest of the world. In most places in Norway it had gone out of use by 1930, but in Setesdal it was practiced well into the 1950s.

The *reivebarn* (swaddled baby) was dressed in a linen or cotton shirt and jacket and then wrapped—first in several layers of soft, absorbent cloth or rags (usually made from cast-off adult clothing), and then with a larger outer cloth

Fig. 20: Doll dressed in traditional swaddling clothes with pick-up swaddling band, from Setesdal in Aust-Agder, 1935. *Photo: Anna Grostøl/Norsk Folkemuseum.*

Fig. 21: Gurine Engedal carrying swaddled baby in sling to christening, Vest-Agder,1941.
Photo: Anna Grostøl/Norsk Folkemuseum.

of wool (which retains heat even when wet). A long band, called the *linde* or *lindeband* (swaddling band), was wrapped around and around the outer cloth from feet to shoulders, to fasten the clothes in place and restrict movement so the baby became a neat little bundle. The ends of the band were secured by tucking them under adjacent rounds.

Swaddling kept babies calmer and less likely to cry. It also added warmth and protection, especially important during the night when houses were unheated and drafty. The band held all the layers in place, keeping the baby cleaner and the bed dry. Swaddled babies were also safer—not only because they couldn't fall out of a bed without sides but because they couldn't wriggle out of their mother's or siblings' arms or out of the woven *bærelinde* (sling or carrying band) as they were carried around during the workday. Most babies were swaddled until they were four to six months old. But some continued to be swaddled at night as a way to keep them warm, even until they were as old as two years.

When used to clothe a baby for christening, the swaddling band was called the *kristenband* (christening band). Because of the importance of the occasion, only the finest woven bands were used for christenings. In Setesdal, babies were dressed for christening in the same way as for everyday, except that everything was new.

Fig. 22: Woman carrying baby to christening, with pick-up band wrapped around white outer cloth, Sør-Trøndelag, 1914.
Photo: Hans Dedekam/Norsk Folkemuseum.

If the swaddled baby was wrapped with an outer layer—a blanket or coverlet for everyday or a fine white cloth or *kristenbløye* for christening—it was held in place by a narrower patterned band called the *bløyeband*. Author Nicolai Ramm Østgaard (1812–1873) referred to a *bløyeband* when he described a baptismal ceremony he attended as an eight-year-old boy in the Tynset church in Nord-Østerdalen, where the baby was carried forth *"i sine hvide Liinsvøb omviklede med de røde Baand"* (in its white linen cloth wrapped around with the red band).[15]

Swaddling bands were usually about 1¼–2" wide. The length varied between 3¼–4½ yards depending on the width and method of wrapping. All of the different bandweaving techniques known in Norway were used for swaddling bands, but pick-up was especially common and appears to have been used for some of the finest examples.

In the 1960s, Eilif Steinsland from Modalen, Hordaland, participated in a national project to gather memories of folk customs from those born before 1900. He remembered details about pick-up weaving and the bandgrind from his childhood and said, *"Å laga lindar var noko av eit kunstverk, og det var ikkje alle som lærde det"* (Weaving swaddling bands was something of an art, and it was not everyone who learned it).[16]

As with bands for adult costumes, the patterns and colors were often characteristic of the locale and could reinforce a sense of regional identity. In Setesdal, an everyday swaddling band might be woven in plain weave while those for christening and important occasions would be woven with a pick-up pattern. These pick-up swaddling bands were similar to the belts used in the Setesdal women's costume in color, pattern, and materials but they were longer and narrower.

Inger Lise Christie identified five methods of wrapping a swaddling band used in Norway.[17] The oldest, used until the late 1600s, was the crisscross method in which a narrow band was wrapped in a widely-spaced crisscross pattern. The diagonal method was documented in Scandinavia from the mid-1600s to the beginning of the 1800s, and the circular method was documented in Scandinavia in the 1800s and later. Both the diagonal and circular methods typically used wider bands, either sewn from cloth or knitted, and had closely-spaced rounds that sometimes overlapped.

Two variations of earlier methods appeared in the 1800s. These variations used some circular rounds around the ankles to hold the band in place and some widely-spaced diagonal rounds up to the chest. In one, the arms were folded over the chest instead of laid at the sides and the band was crossed over the chest. In another, there were some circular rounds instead of a cross over the chest. If the arms were left loose the two methods looked the same.

These two later variations were associated with narrow woven bands, often woven in pick-up. They were used in the more isolated, conservative districts—like the upper areas of the eastern valleys of Telemark and Buskerud, the inner districts of Agder, such as Setesdal, and the fjord districts of western Norway and Trøndelag—where pick-up traditions were strong.

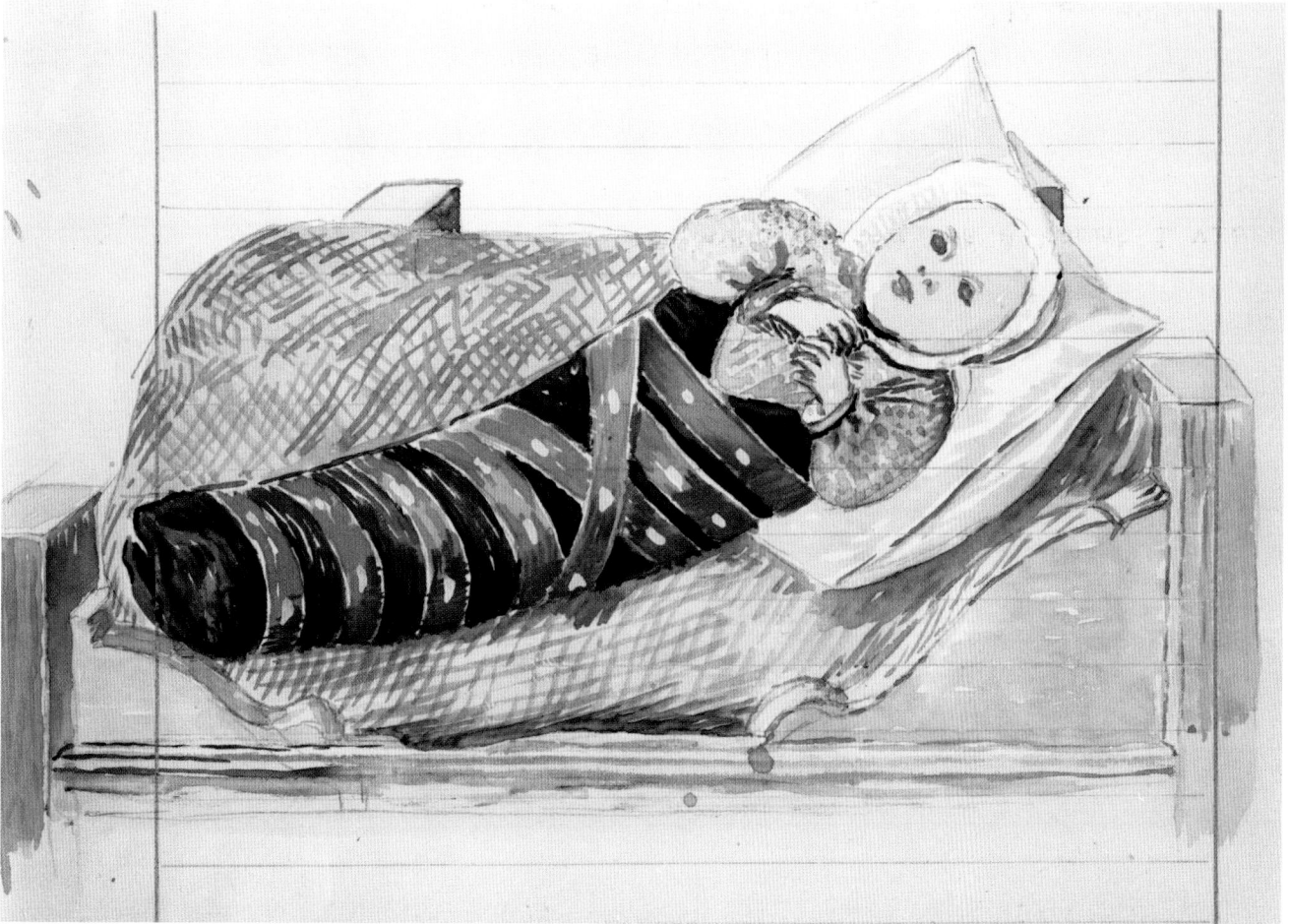

Fig. 23: Drawing showing swaddling method with arms left free, Hordaland. *Photo: Knut Spjeldnes/Norsk Folkemuseum.*

The diagonal and circular methods, which used wider sewn bands, were used in districts with good contact with cities, government officials, and trade routes—like Oslo, Rogaland and Nord-Trøndelag—where folk dress traditions went out of use early and woven swaddling bands have not been preserved.

According to Christie, the more widely-spaced methods of wrapping that used narrow woven bands were primarily a means of clothing the baby, while the closely-spaced methods that used wider cloth bands were often associated with the idea that swaddling helped to properly form and straighten the legs, arms, and back as the baby grew. This idea had been propounded by some experts in Europe since ancient times but apparently came later to Norway.[18]

Eventually this idea intermingled with other perceptions about swaddling and was commonly cited as a reason for swaddling even in areas like Buskerud that used the narrower bands. This is illustrated by responses to the *Norsk Etnologisk Gransking* (Norwegian Ethnological Study, Norsk Folkemuseum), which posed questions in the 1950s about swaddling practices as people remembered them. A response from Sigdal in Buskerud said, *"Vess ongen vart hjulbeint, hadde døm snørt lista for løst, sa døm"* (If the young one was bowlegged, they had bound the swaddling band too loosely, it was said).[19]

A response from Uvdal in Buskerud said that having the arms in kept the baby warm and described the wrapping as beginning near the feet: *"Ein gong ront anklerne to gange rundt knerne so ikkje onjin skulde bli julbeint. Krøsband aaver skulderen, teslutt omkring magan."* (One time around the ankles, two times around the knees so the child won't be bowlegged. Cross the band over the shoulders, finally around the stomach.) It went on to say that as the baby grew the swaddling could be done looser and the cross over the shoulders omitted, apparently then leaving the arms free.[20]

Beginning in the 1600s, some European doctors began to form new ideas about child rearing and began to speak out against swaddling. In spite of this, the old traditions continued to be passed from one generation to the next. In Norway, as late as the first decades of the 1900s, midwives were still being taught to swaddle babies, although by this time the custom was to not include the arms.

Folk Beliefs

Swaddling bands and christening bands were seen as having magical powers of protection. In rural Norway, ancient folk beliefs about evil forces and how to protect against them did not disappear with the coming of Christianity. Instead, those folk beliefs intermingled with Christian beliefs and continued to influence people's lives for hundred of years. This did not change until the second half of the 1800s, when widespread education and modern ways of thinking became established in the rural areas.

Before baptism the child was thought to be especially susceptible to threats from the supernatural world. The biggest fear was that the child would be replaced with a *bytting* (changeling)—the misshapen or unhealthy offspring of *huldrefolk* (hidden folk), also called *underjordiske* (underworld folk).

The underworld folk were invisible creatures who were constantly lurking about farm buildings and mountain pastures and could appear in human form. For them, stealing healthy babies was a way to improve their bloodlines. For rural Norwegians, changeling legends were a way of explaining what happened when a formerly healthy baby developed rickets or another illness.

As late as the 1950s in Alvdal in Nord-Østerdalen, some people still repeated the belief that an unbaptised baby should not be taken up to the remote summer pastures in the mountains where the dangers from underworld folk were especially great.[21]

Baptism was believed to be the most important protection from such dangers. Consequently, the baptismal journey to the parish church was undertaken as soon as possible, often when the baby was only a few days old and often over rough terrain in inclement weather, even though the baby was vulnerable to the rigors of the journey and to underworld folk along the way.

Swaddling bands were one means of protecting a baby. Thought to ward off evil, red was used as the main color. Diagonal cross motifs in many variations were woven in pick-up, since the cross was a powerful protective symbol.

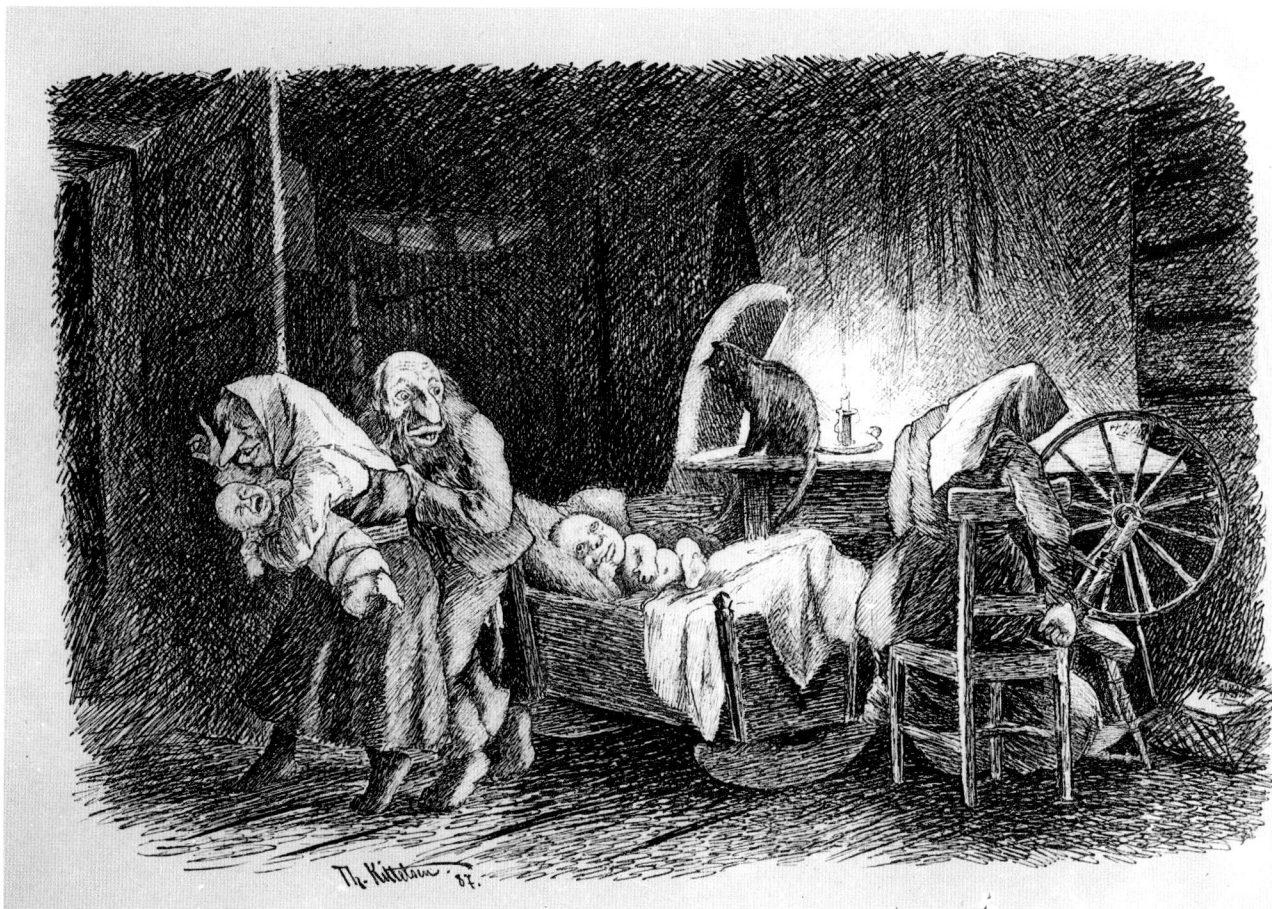

Fig. 24: Theodor Kittelsen, (1857–1914), untitled drawing, 1887. The mother has fallen asleep at her spinning wheel and the underworld folk have stolen in to replace her healthy baby with a misshapen one of their own.
Photo©: O. Væring Eftf. AS.

Letters of the alphabet were sometimes used as motifs because they were credited with magical powers, like the ancient runes before them had been. According to Christie, one tradition held that pick-up motifs should be varied and not repeated exactly over the whole length of the band.[22]

In Setesdal, wrapping the band ended with a cross over the chest and it was said, *"Krossmerket verna barnet mot tussar og andre underjordiske"* (The sign of the cross protected the baby against underworld folk).[23]

Silver and steel were believed to have magical powers of protection, and silver coins or small metal objects were often sewn into the baby's clothing. The ends of christening bands were sometimes finished with a facing of red wool cloth, and a coin or other metal object would be tucked underneath before it was sewn in place.

The numbers three and seven were also thought to have magical powers of protection. In Østerdalen it was said, *"Linden skulle vera 7 alner lang, korkje meir eller mindre. Elles kunne det hende noko gali med barnet. I eine enden skulle det vera innsauma ein sølvskilling og i andre enden skulle det vera ei nål."* (The swaddling band should be 7 alner [14 feet] long, neither more nor less. Otherwise something bad could happen to the child. In one end there should be sewn a silver coin and in the other end there should be a needle.)[24]

Fig. 25: Woman getting ready to carry porridge container and sending basket, both wrapped with pick-up bands, on shoulder yoke, Oppland.
Photo: Norsk Folkemuseum.

And also from Østerdalen, "*Når ein skulde linde barnet, laut ein akte på å sveipe linden 3 gonger rundt nedafor kneet, berre ein gong rundt låret, 3 gonger rundt livet. Så skulde ein linde armane så linden låg i kors over ryggen og bringa.*" (When one swaddles the child, care should be taken to wrap the swaddling band 3 times around below the knees, only one time around the thighs, 3 times around the waist. Then one should swaddle the arms so the band lies in a cross over the back and the chest.)[25]

Another mention of the number three and the sign of the cross comes from Sogn og Fjordane, where the trip to church for the christening was often a mile or more. The mother did not often make the journey because she had just given birth, so a nursemaid would carry the baby, and to ease the burden on her arms she could use a pick-up *bærelinde* (sling or carrying band). It was said that the band should be three meters long (about 3¼ yards) and knotted so it formed a cross over the woman's back.[26]

Christening clothes were even thought to have healing powers later in life, so a christening band with a pattern of crosses and metal sewn into the ends might be brought out to help cure a sick child.

Sending Baskets

In the old days, farms belonged to a *belag*, a group of neighboring farms that mutually invited one another to important or festive gatherings, like weddings. Contributions of food from every family in the belag were necessary in order to feed guests, since the farm hosting the event usually did not have resources to do so on its own. The saying *granne skal granne hjelpa* (neighbor shall help neighbor) summed up the function of the belag as a support system, with each farm giving and receiving in turn.

A contribution of baked goods was sent in a *sendingskorg* (sending basket, at right in Fig. 27), tied up with a pick-up *sendingsband* (sending band). There were local variations of the sending basket, but most were round in shape and did not have lids. Some baskets were woven from birch root with openwork around the top. Others were made from a thin strip of wood formed into a circle, neatly lashed together at the ends and set onto a wooden bottom. A wooden basket might be decorated with painted designs and the initials of the woman who owned it.

A contribution of *fløtegrøt* or *rømmegrøt* (sweet cream porridge or sour cream porridge) was sent in a wooden vessel called an *ambar* or *grautspann* (porridge pail, at left in Fig. 27) that had a lid. Such porridge is a Norwegian delicacy and was commonly taken not only to festive gatherings but to women who had just given birth.

The sending basket was lined with a white cloth and filled with baked goods that were traditional for the particular district. The cloth was then folded over the top and tied in place with a sending band that served both to secure the package and decorate it. The porridge pail could also be tied up with a sending band.

Fig. 26: Drawing of pick-up pattern used in sending band from Møre og Romsdal.

Fig. 27: Porridge container and sending basket, wrapped with pick-up bands, Oppland. *Photo: Norsk Folkemuseum.*

A writer described a sending band from Møre og Romsdal like this: "*Et vevd rödtavla 'sendingsbann' hörte också med til utstyret. Det var vevd på ei bandgrind, og hadde fine röde og hvite dusker i endene.*" (A woven red-checked sending band also belonged to the sending outfit. It was woven on a bandgrind and had fine red and white tassels at the ends.) This particular band was ¾" wide and 121" long and its checked or hatched pattern is shown in Fig. 26.[27]

Wedding celebrations in the old farm society typically lasted two or three days and the contributions of food had to be sufficient to feed the guests over this time. The size of the sending basket and its contents depended on the relative means of the family sending the contribution, so that a wife from a large farm had a larger basket and sent more food than the wife of a cotter.

When the event was over, each sending basket and porridge pail, with its respective band, would be brought back home, often with leftover bits of food for the ones who had to stay home to tend the animals. It is easy to imagine that the beautiful sending bands provided a means of identifying to whom each basket belonged and were a source of pride at these events for the farm wives who owned them.

The Husflid Movement

Around the mid-1800s, rural Norwegian society began to change. The first railway lines were built. New, mechanized farming methods were introduced. Trade restrictions were lifted. The new country stores offered a variety of cheap, imported goods to compete with locally-produced, handcrafted ones. A primarily money-based economy came to rural Norway for the first time.

All of this changed the way farm families spent their time. Skills stopped being passed from one generation to the next and gradually the old *husflid* (folk craft or home craft) traditions began to die. Farm wives passed off the household weaving to cotters' wives and servants. Later, machine-woven cotton began to replace linen in most homes. Handweaving as a common skill became a thing of the past in many areas.

Hildeborg Sagneskar of Valle in Setesdal, who was born in 1894, told Aagot Noss in 1965, "*Før måtte kver vever for seg sjølv, men det minkar allfort*" (Before, everyone had to weave for themselves, but that dwindled steadily).[28]

In the 1870s, a movement began to preserve the old skills. Sociologist Eilert Sundt (1817–1875) has been called the father of the husflid movement. In his 1868 book, *Om Husfliden i Norge* (On Home Crafts in Norway), he promoted the idea of using the traditional crafts as a way to fight widespread unemployment and poverty. Other activists and educators followed in his footsteps and formed organizations and schools. The idea was to help people by providing a way for them to help themselves—to teach them traditional crafts and provide an outlet where they could sell their products.

Fig. 28: Group portrait, men and women outside Norsk Husflids Skole, Oslo.
Photo: Ludvig Forbech/Norsk Folkemuseum.

Throughout the 1800s, there was a growing nationalism in Norway. After having been governed by Denmark for over 400 years, Norway declared its independence in 1814, only to be forced into a union with Sweden before finally gaining independence in 1905. A growing sense of national pride created an interest in everything that was considered typically Norwegian, including folk arts and crafts.

In the 1880s, several organizations were formed to preserve rural folk arts and crafts. In 1891 three of them merged to form *Den Norske Husflidsforening* (The Norwegian Home Crafts Association), which opened a Husfliden store in Oslo in 1892 for the sale of traditional craft items from rural areas.

In 1904, Den Norske Husflidsforening published *Haandbog i vævning*, later re-spelled *Håndbok i vevning* (Handbook in Weaving), which went on to be printed in many editions for more than half a century. It was both a how-to book, with instructions for weaving on a floor loom, and a pattern book, with specifications for a variety of textiles. The chapter on bandweaving briefly summarizes the process of weaving on two different kinds of band looms and includes patterns for several kinds of bands, including pick-up.[29]

Until World War II, Den Norske Husflidsforening held regular weaving courses that met for eight hours a day and lasted for two months, in which students learned how to use a floor loom and weave dress goods, household linens, and decorative textiles. They also learned bandweaving.

Later, bandweaving classes were offered by Husfliden shops and local organizations. How-to booklets became available, but some still learned the craft in the old way. In the 1960s in Setesdal and Telemark, there were still some older women weaving pick-up bands who had learned the craft from their mothers, part of an unbroken line of knowledge and tradition passed down through the generations.

The Bunad Movement

Some of the bandweaving patterns and techniques that survived for hundreds of years in rural folk dress have been preserved in today's *bunader* (regional costumes, based on traditional church-going clothes, worn by modern Norwegians for special occasions, singular *bunad*).

By the end of the 1800s, rural Norwegians were adopting fashionable "town wear" and folk dress traditions were dying out. A simplified version of the costume from Hardanger was often used as a national costume for festive occasions and folk dance groups. Then interest grew in preserving other rural costumes and the bunad movement took hold. Over time, work began in many districts to revive, reconstruct, and develop festive regional costumes for modern use, a process that continues today.

Hulda Garborg (1862–1934) wrote the first bunad book in Norway, *Norsk Klædebunad* (Norwegian Traditional Dress), in 1903 and was an early pioneer in the movement. As a member of a popular folk dance group, she promoted the use of folk costumes for folk dancing, and people began to feel that it was better to

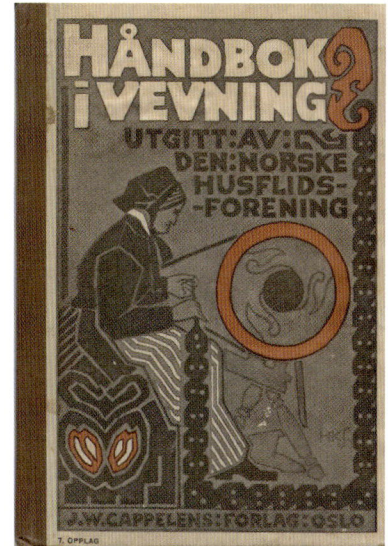

Fig. 29: Weaving handbook published by *Den Norske Husflidsforening* (The Norwegian Home Crafts Association), ©*Cappelen Damm AS, Norway*. Photo: Author.

Fig. 30: Traditional dress from Sauland, Øst-Telemark, presumably from second half of 1800s, when the *beltestakk*, or skirt with wide tablet-woven belt, was popular. The bunad known as the beltestakk today was developed from existing dresses such as this one.
Photo: Vesterheim (Luther College Collection 4293).

Fig. 31: Bunad from Åmli in Aust-Agder, made in Norway in 1967.
Photo: Vesterheim (2003.42.1).

wear a costume from one's home district than a copy of the Hardanger dress. But Garborg advocated making changes to folk dress and not everyone agreed with her approach. She did not believe in using imported cloth, even though such cloth had been used in the old days. According to Aagot Noss, Garborg promoted the use of wool embroidery on woolen cloth so much that in some districts it replaced the variety of decoration, including bands and ribbons, that had been known before.[30]

Later, Klara Semb (1884–1970) was also active in folk dancing and was an important leader in the bunad movement until she retired in 1965. Unlike Hulda Garborg, she believed that the old folk dress should be meticulously copied and not changed. This goal of authenticity became an underlying principle in the bunad movement.

Klara Semb was a member of the *Landsnemnda for Bunadspørsmål*, established in 1947 and renamed *Bunad- og folkedraktrådet* (Norwegian Council for Folk Costumes) in 1986. This advisory panel is composed of experts in cultural history, folk costumes, textiles, and sewing. It answers questions on the use, history, and reconstruction of bunader. It also reports on proposed bunader that are submitted to it for review and how well they represent the local folk dress traditions of a particular time and place.

In Setesdal, folk dress never went completely out of use, so the bunad there is simply the folk dress as it existed at the time interest in bunader grew—folk dress that took on a new role.

In other places, the bunad was based on folk dress that had gone out of use but was not forgotten. And in still other places the bunad had to be reconstructed, based on preserved old folk dress items and supplemented with written information, pictures, and oral traditions. Sometimes there was not enough source material on which to draw and some or all of the pieces were newly designed. But many of the bunader that include pick-up bands are from rural areas with well-preserved folk dress traditions, and bandweaves are one of the oldest techniques preserved in bunader.

If much source material was available a bunad might have several variations. The Åmli bunad from Aust-Agder, for example, preserved many of the small differences that existed within the area, and there are five patterns to choose from for the pick-up belt. Some counties, like Telemark, have different bunader for the many communities within the county and for different time periods. In Tinn in Telemark there are two bunader, one representing the early 1800s and one representing the mid-1800s, both with pick-up apron bands.

But the variety available in bunader is still very limited when compared to folk dress. A band made for a particular bunad today, for example, will likely always have exactly the same color and pattern, whereas in the old days the color and pattern could vary somewhat from person to person while the overall style stayed the same.

Today, pick-up bands are used in either some or all of the bunader from these counties: Aust-Agder, Buskerud, Hordaland, Sogn og Fjordane, Telemark, Vest-Agder, and Vestfold. Many Norwegian women own a bunad and wear

Fig. 32: Tora B. Kvestad, Setesdal in Aust-Agder. The folk costume in Setesdal never went completely out of use and later took on a new role as a bunad for festive occasions.
Photo: Vesterheim, Harstad Collection.

it proudly for special occasions like baptisms, confirmations, weddings, and public celebrations like *Syttende mai* (May 17th, Norwegian Constitution Day). Unlike regular clothing, bunader never go out of style, are kept for a lifetime, and are handed down to the next generation.

Strong cultural conventions influence the use of the bunad. To preserve historical accuracy and regional identities bunader are not supposed to be varied or to evolve, like folk costumes did naturally in the old society, because then they would begin to conform more to modern tastes and norms and cease to be representations of folk dress as it existed in a certain time and place.

Fig. 33: Classic Fana sweater, trimmed with red and white pick-up bands, purchased in Norway in 1951. *Photo: Vesterheim (1978.27.1).*

Fana Sweaters

Pick-up bands were also used to trim sweaters from Fana in Hordaland near Bergen. The distinctive striped Fana sweaters have been traced back to the mid-1800s and were originally used by men for everyday wear. In the 1930s girls began to use them for casual wear, and by the time of the 1952 Olympics in Oslo they were popular as ski sweaters with both men and women all over the country.

These cardigan-style sweaters are knitted in two colors of wool—usually natural white with brown, black, dark blue, or grey. The oldest examples were solid white below the chest where they were tucked into trousers, but later examples are patterned all over. The sweater body is knitted in alternating light and dark stripes with contrasting flecks or small designs. A checkerboard pattern is knitted at the bottom edge, with borders of *åttebladsroser* (eight-petaled roses) above the checkerboard and at the shoulders, cuffs, and tops of the sleeves. Some sweaters use fewer borders, some more. Buttons are silver or pewter.

Narrow woven bands, called *kvardeband* (edging bands) in the dialect of the region, serve not only as decorative trim but to strengthen and stabilize the edges of the garment at the front opening and around the neckline and cuffs. The band is sewn to the edge of the sweater along with a fabric facing on the inside. Sometimes the band is folded over the edge, other times it is sewn even with the edge or a little offset over the edge. Bands in pick-up are common, often in red wool pattern on a background of white cotton. Other colors, like brown, black, yellow, and green, are also used. The bands are narrow, usually just over a half inch or so.

Another Fana sweater that uses bands for edging is the men's white sweater. It is knitted in natural white homespun in garter stitch, with knit/purl patterns on the bottom edge, cuffs, and sometimes the shoulders. Narrow bands trim the neckline, front opening, and cuffs as with the striped sweater. The white sweater is believed to be older than the two-color striped sweater and has apparently always been worn only by men and only for Sunday best. Originally this sweater was worn tucked into blue wool trousers with embroidered suspenders on top. It was common until about 1920, when folk dress for men began to decline. Today, some men wear white sweaters outside the trousers like a regular cardigan.

Coverlets and Cushion Covers

In the late 1970s and early 1980s, a group of old *langputer* (long cushions) and one *bandåkle* (band coverlet), all made by sewing bands together, were registered by Torbjørg Gauslaa.

A langpute is a long pillow or cushion that fits the width of a narrow bed or the seat of a horse-drawn sleigh or buggy. See Fig. 35. A bandåkle is a type of *fellåkle*, a woven coverlet sewn to the leather side of a sheepskin pelt. Cushions

Fig. 34: Detail of coverlet made by Kiersti Halvorsdatter Rø in 1849, of 44 pick-up bands sewn together, from Vingelen in Nord-Østerdalen.
Photo: Norsk Folkemuseum.

and coverlets were usually made from wider handwoven cloth, so these band textiles are unusual. They were made in the 1800s, and most are from Nord-Østerdalen and nearby Røros in Sør-Trøndelag.

All of the bands are pick-up with the exception of a couple of tablet-woven and knitted bands. They are whipstitched together from the wrong side with linen yarn. Some bands appear to have been woven specifically for use in these larger textiles. Others were sewn together only after they had served another purpose. For example, bands that appear in a cushion in matching pairs, each band with fringe at only one end, were likely originally used for stocking bands.

The coverlet shown in Fig. 34 is about 50" wide and 67" long and displays a high level of competence in both design and weaving technique. It was woven by Kiersti Halvorsdatter Rø (1794 or 1795–1874). According to Gauslaa, people in the area remembered stories about Kiersti, a talented woman, good with her hands, who never married and was a prolific weaver. When she was twenty years old she fell from a barn loft and injured her hip, and for the rest of her life needed help to get around. She had a difficult life, but her weaving shows that she found interest and satisfaction in her craft.[31]

Six of the bands in the coverlet have woven-in text. The letters and numbers are elegantly designed. Two text bands near the top contain what Gauslaa refers to as a *skjemterim* (jesting rhyme). It isn't clear who the message was for, but it shows that Kiersti had a sense of humor.[32] "*GJØR MIG EN MAGE OG SKIK M MIG DEN TIL BAGE DIN SKARV*" (Make me a match and send it back to me you rascal) and "*DETTE STYKKE ER JORT I MIT 55 AAR DEN FØRSTE NOVEMBER 1849 KIERSTI HALVORSDATTER RØ I VINGELEN*" (This piece is done in my 55th year the first of November 1849 Kiersti Halvorsdatter Rø in Vingelen).

Fig. 35: Cushion cover made by sewing pick-up bands together, Røros, Sør-Trøndelag.
Photo: Anne-Lise Reinsfelt/Norsk Folkemuseum.

Fig. 36: Pick-up band with woven-in name and date, Ragnhild Lømo, 1903 on one end, RL, 1903 on the other.
Photo: Glomdalsmuseet.

Kiersti's coverlet was originally sewn to a sheepskin pelt, as is common with Norwegian coverlets, and there are remnants of linen sewing thread around the outsides edges. But it was also used alone as a coverlet without the sheepskin layer. A few other band coverlets were known in the area. One woman told Gauslaa that she remembered a small band coverlet that had been kept in a made-up cradle, possibly on top of a quilt or sheepskin, at a farm in Os in Nord-Østerdalen that was destroyed by fire in 1940.[33] A baby coverlet made by Olea Gjermundsdatter Lyseggen from Trysil was mentioned above in the section on Textile Traditions (see Fig. 13).

In Sweden at the Jämtland county museum there are two so-called "musicians' coverlets" from Härjedalen county in Sweden, sewn from bands collected by Swedish fiddlers who played at weddings and received the bands as gifts from the brides. One is dated 1771. Jämtland and Härjedalen counties lie east of Nord-Østerdalen and until the mid-1600s were part of Norway.

Woven-in Initials and Dates

The coverlet is the only one of these wider band textiles with a woven-in message, but five of the cushions have initials and four have dates (1837,1844, 1844, and 1848). In one cushion the initials SPS stand for Simon Pedersen Nygaard (1849–1927). His granddaughter remembered the cushion from her grandparents' bed and how heavy it had been to take outside and beat on cleaning days.[34]

The custom of weaving in initials and dates on bands was not uncommon. Usually the initials were those of the owner of the piece, even if it was woven by someone else. One of the band cushions contains the inscription PESB 1844 and is believed to have been woven by Kiersti Halvorsdatter Rø for her nephew, Per Eriksen Berg (1821–1899).[35]

It was rare for a professional weaver of domestic textiles to sign work made for another, but that appears to have been done in a group of ten bands from Østerdalen that were studied by Inger Lise Christie. All were finely made and had many characteristics in common. Christie believes they were used as christening bands.[36]

Three have woven-in dates: 1787, 1791, and 1807. All of the bands have initials, either those of a woman, such as AHD, where the D stands for *datter* (daughter), or those of a couple, such as BBS AED, where the S stands for *sønn* (son). These are presumed to be the owners' initials. According to the rural naming conventions of the time, a person's given name was followed by a patronym consisting of the father's name plus datter for females and sønn for males.

Some of the bands also have a second set of initials and some of those have a farm name after the second set of initials, as in KPD Meselt. See Fig. 37. Since the same second set of initials appears on bands for different owners and the bands evidence a high degree of technical proficiency, Christie believes that the weavers might have been specialists in the craft who sold and did indeed sign their work.[37]

Christie's research into parish records reveals that IOD could stand for Ingeborg Olsdatter (1744–1814), a widow who lived on a cotter's place on the Stai farm for many years and might have woven to supplement her income. KPD could stand for Kari Pedersdatter (1780–1845), the daughter of Ingeborg Olsdatter, who was born at Stai and moved to the neighboring farm of Meselt after she married. It was common for both men and women to add the name of the farm where they lived after their name and to change that farm name when they moved, which would explain why one band bears the name KPD Stai and two bear the name KPD Meselt.[38]

Fig. 37: Pick-up band with woven-in initials and a farm name, BBS AED on one end, KPD Meselt on the other.
Photo: Glomdalsmuseet.

The Røros Market

Today it is possible to see pick-up coat bands at the winter market in the town of Røros in Sør-Trøndelag. In a re-creation of old market traditions, dozens of drivers with horse-drawn sleds travel from neighboring regions to the market in traditional dress from the 1700s–1800s.

The market began in Røros in the late 1600s, after a copper mine started production there in 1644. In those days there were few roads and it was easiest to transport goods in the winter by horse and sled, across snow and ice. People came to the winter market with goods to sell and trade from the surrounding areas in Norway and Sweden. In the beginning a law prohibited the market, but this was largely ignored and finally, in the mid-1800s, a government decree officially designated a period in February for the market to be held each year.

There were strong traditions of pick-up weaving in some of the areas of Sweden that participated in the Røros market. We don't know if pick-up bands were an item of trade, but the market could have contributed to the exchange of weaving patterns through the coat bands worn by the sled drivers. And some of the horses themselves might have worn pick-up bands, since bands used for reins and to hold horse blankets in place have been found in the area.

Similar Traditions from Other Lands

Pick-up weaving was known not only in Norway and Sweden, but in other countries that had traditional farm cultures, like Lithuania, Latvia, Estonia, and Finland. Different places developed distinct styles of color and pattern, but at the same time there are natural similarities in the motifs used throughout the region. Since pick-up motifs are an outgrowth of the weave structure and technique, many similar patterns probably developed independently from place to place. But there was also a sharing of ideas, as traders and travelers brought textiles from other lands. Some communities made bands for sale, and their work might have had a more widespread influence.

In *Swedish Handcraft*, Anna-Maja Nylén writes that in Dalarna county in Sweden, "bands of remarkable quality and in considerable quantities were made in several parishes. In Garsås village in Mora parish, manufacture for sale was extensive. The women sold patterned bands to other Dalarna parishes as well as outside the province." She also notes that bands were among the most common wares sold by itinerant peddlers.[39] Weavers seeing bands from other regions might be inspired by new ideas, adapting motifs according to local preferences and then varying them further over time.

There are also similarities in the traditions surrounding the use of pick-up bands in these countries. In Sweden, for example, bands were used as apron bands, swaddling bands, coat bands, and carrying bands, and the bride gave gifts of bands at her wedding just as she did in Norway. In Finland, pick-up bands were used for many items including belts and horse reins and were also given as bride's presents to the groom's relatives.

In Lithuania, a young girl learned pick-up weaving from her mother, grandmother, or older sister and wove dozens of colorful sashes to fill her dowry chest. When she received a handcrafted weaving tool from her suitor as a courting gift, she gave him a sash in return. At her wedding, she presented sashes to the groom's relatives and people like the matchmaker and the coachman who were part of the celebration. When she gave birth, she wrapped a special sash around the baby at the christening ceremony.

Throughout the region, pick-up weaving was a respected craft and sign of a young woman's skill.

Immigration to America

Over a period of about a hundred years, beginning in 1825, over 800,000 Norwegians left their ancestral homeland and immigrated to America. The emigration began in the wake of a population increase brought about in part by improved sanitation, the smallpox vaccine, and a better diet that included potatoes. In a country where only about 3% of the land is farmland, there was a growing class of poor rural folk who had few prospects. America held the promise of a better future.

When the emigration began, the society in rural Norway was much the same as it had been for hundreds of years. Traditional folk dress was still worn and babies were still swaddled. Many emigrants came from isolated valleys and fjord areas where weaving traditions were strong, and pick-up bands were often included in the belongings they took with them.

Many also packed bandgrinder for the journey. Vesterheim Norwegian-American Museum in Decorah, Iowa, has about two dozen in its collection. The oldest is dated 1763. Perhaps bandgrinder were included because they had been courting gifts and had sentimental value and were easy to tuck into the wooden trunk that held the family's possessions, and perhaps the women intended to continue bandweaving in the new land. The museum notes in a display that although bandgrinder were often included with the household goods brought from Norway, there is little evidence they were used by the immigrants in America.

As soon as the immigrants arrived, many of their social customs began to change. Not wanting to appear foreign, they usually adopted American dress as soon as they were able. The changes even extended to the way babies were dressed. According to Laurann Gilbertson and Carol Colburn, "Many immigrant families discontinued the use of swaddling bands for infants in America, adopting the American custom of dressing infants in small shifts instead."[40]

The custom of swaddling, although no longer practiced, was remembered even several generations later. Gertrude Berg, a third-generation Norwegian-American, donated some family heirlooms to Vesterheim in 1984, including a band brought from Sogn in 1867. In a letter to Vesterheim she said, "As far as I know, such bands were woven especially to hold the wraps on youngsters. This was before safety pins were invented."[41]

Not all pick-up bands were immediately set aside in favor of simpler accessories. Gilbertson and Colburn note that they were "sometimes used in America with fashionable dress, as applied trim or as colorful neck bows or ties for children."[42] And many Norwegian-Americans who did not continue to wear traditional clothing for everyday wear were proud to wear some form of it for public occasions like dances, parades, and meetings of groups like the Sons of Norway. This was especially true after the late 1800s, when Norway's revival of folk dress and the bunad movement took hold in America too.

Even those who no longer used their bands saved them and passed them down to succeeding generations. Those who inherited the bands did not always know what they had been used for, but kept them as keepsakes and symbols of nostalgia for the old homeland. Dozens of these bands survived to end up in Vesterheim's textile collection and we'll look at some of them in **Part 2**.

Fig. 39: Øst-Telemark dress that belonged to Anne Jonsdatter Gutukjær (1834–1915). Anne wore the dress for her second marriage in Norway around 1875, and brought it with her when she and her family immigrated to the Dakota Territory in 1887.
Photo: Vesterheim (1971.13.1).

Fig. 40: Bandgrind, initials R R painted on top piece, year 1795 in partially illegible carving on bottom piece. Many bandgrinder were brought to this country by Norwegian immigrants.
Photo: Vesterheim (1975.52.1).

Bandweaving Looms

Textile work was women's work in rural Norway, as it had been from ancient times. The sagas tell tales of men who did women's work meeting with scorn and disdain. But making looms and other textiles tools from wood was traditionally a man's contribution.

A description of a man and wife from *Rigsthula* in the *Poetic Edda*, thought to date from the first half of the 10th century, reflects this division of labor. While the man "hewed wood for the weaver's beam," the woman "at the weaving with arms outstretched she worked."[43]

Pick-up weaving is a hand-manipulated technique, so it can be done on almost any loom that produces two sheds. Large floor looms that are used for weaving cloth can also be used for bandweaving, and they sometimes were in Norway. But smaller looms specifically designed for the purpose are often more convenient.

In Norway, there were three main kinds of looms made specifically for bandweaving. The most widespread was the *bandgrind* (hole-and-slot band heddle, plural *bandgrinder*). It was known in all parts of Norway except Setesdal. Two other types had a more local distribution. One was the *bandvevrei* or *bandstøre*, vertical frame looms from Setesdal and Telemark respectively. The third was the *bandstol* (band loom), somewhat similar to the English inkle loom, used in eastern Norway.

Band Heddle

The bandgrind or band heddle is an ancient and simple weaving tool. It consists of a series of bars in a frame. Each bar has a hole in its center and is separated from neighboring bars by a space or slot. A bandgrind can be carved from a single piece of wood, like the one shown in Fig. 41, or the bars can be made separately and fastened to top and bottom crosspieces.

Fig. 41: Bandgrind, carved from one piece of oak.
Photo: Vesterheim (Luther College Collection 1398).

Basic Weaving Terms

For non-weavers, here is a quick primer on the weaving terms used to describe the traditional Norwegian band looms. For more detailed information, see **Part 3**.

A woven band is created when a set of lengthwise threads called the **warp** is interlaced at right angles with a crosswise thread called the **weft**. The **warp** is placed on a **loom**, which holds the warp under tension and has a means to raise and lower alternate warp threads to create spaces or **sheds** for the weft to pass through. On the bandgrind the warp is threaded through the holes and slots and the sheds are made simply by moving the bandgrind up and down. On other looms **heddles** made from loops of string are part of the shedding system. The weft is wound onto a wooden tool called a **shuttle**, which is used to carry the weft through the shed and pack the weft into place.

The bandgrind is most often used in a simple backstrap arrangement, in which the warp is held under tension by fastening one end to a belt around the weaver's waist and the other end to a solid object in front of the weaver, like a bedpost or tree. The bandgrinder pictured in this book, many likely given as courting gifts, have enough holes and slots for 33–55 threads. Wider bandgrinder, for 60–80 threads, were common, and a few could accommodate as many as 100 or 120 threads.

In a local variation of bandweaving loom from Sør-Trøndelag, shown in Fig. 43, the bandgrind is mounted in a frame operated with a treadle, allowing the weaver to keep her hands on the work while her feet change sheds.

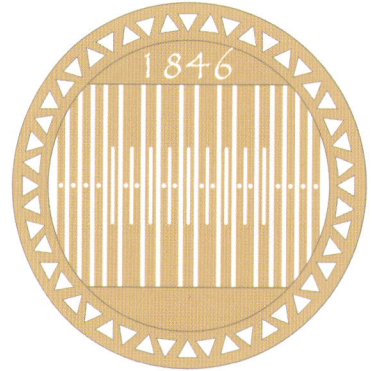

Fig. 42: Drawing of old Finnish *spaltegrind* (hole-and-slot heddle with extra pattern slots).

Fig. 43: Band loom, in which a bandgrind is moved up and down with a foot treadle, made by Johannes Sivertsen Ishol, Sør-Trøndelag.
Photo: Erling Gjone/Norsk Folkemuseum.

Fig. 44: Bandgrind, acanthus carved frame, pegged and dovetailed construction.
Photo: Vesterheim (1985.101.26).

A variation of the bandgrind that is specially designed for weaving one particular kind of pick-up is called a *bandgrind med ekstra mønsterspalter* or *spaltegrind* (band heddle with extra pattern slots, or pattern heddle). It is common today but does not appear to have been used in rural Norway in the old days.

The pattern heddle was apparently popularized by Finnish weaver Barbro Gardberg (1924–2011). When she was growing up, her father found an old, round pattern heddle in a ramshackle shed and hung it on the kitchen wall in the family home. It was carved with decorations and the date 1846. See Fig. 42. Gardberg later researched bandweaving techniques and learned how to use this unusual band heddle. In 1978 an exhibit of her bands and bandweaving tools opened at Västerbottens Museum in Sweden and then traveled to other places in Scandinavia including Nord-Østerdalen in Norway, where she taught a workshop at a museum in 1982.[44]

Some bandgrinder have two or three rows of holes instead of one. These can be used for pick-up weaving, or they can be used along with additional string heddles to weave warp brocade with a supplementary pattern warp, a technique that is outside the scope of this book.

Vertical Band Loom

A different kind of bandweaving loom is used in parts of Setesdal and Telemark. In Setesdal this loom is called the *bandvevrei* and in Telemark it is called the *bandstøre*. See Fig. 45. There are variations, but both are essentially vertical frame looms about 60" high and 24" wide that are supported against a wall or stand upright on a base.

Today some of these looms have two beams with ratchets—a lower beam to hold the woven band and an upper beam to hold the unwoven warp. The older styles have just one beam, the lower one, and the unwoven warp is carried over an upper crosspiece and tightened by a hanging weight or by wrapping around a peg at the side. The loom uses continuous string heddles tied around a heddle rod that remains in a fixed position during weaving, as well as a wooden sword or batten to hold the countershed.

According to Marta Hoffmann, the age of these looms is not known and very few examples have been preserved. There are some dated models from the late 1700s, but the loom could be much older. It is not known whether such looms were used in other countries. Pictures from the Middle Ages depict small, vertical looms but there are not enough details to determine if they operate on the same principles.[45]

Inkle-Style Band Loom

The *bandstol* is another kind of band loom, consisting of a wooden frame, about 40–48" high, with a base, vertical uprights and an upper crosspiece. See Fig. 46. Some have a small box on the upper crosspiece to hold weft yarn and tools.

The loom uses fixed, string heddles like an inkle loom. There are two reels or spools tensioned by ratchets, one on each side of the front upright. The warp is stretched horizontally, from one reel around the opposite upright to the second reel. One reel holds the unwoven warp and the other holds the finished band as it is woven. Some looms have one reel placed on each upright instead of two reels on opposite sides of the same upright.

These looms are known in other parts of Scandinavia and also outside Scandinavia. In Norway they were used in the eastern part of the country, particularly in Oppland and in Hedmark from Stor-Elvdal south. They were not known for the most part in Nord-Østerdalen in northern Hedmark. They were mentioned in the *Furnes Bygdebok* (record book from Furnes in Hedmark) in 1782.[46]

Fig. 46: Petra Hagen weaving on a bandstol, a band loom with fixed heddles, 1938, Oppland.
Photo: Anna Grostøl/Norsk Folkemuseum.

These upright band looms are about the same size and use the same shedding mechanism as English or floor-model inkle looms. But the warp on the inkle loom travels back and forth around a series of pegs to form a continuous loop, rather than being stretched between two reels, and the weaver sits at the end of the loom instead of at the side.

The age of these looms is not known. Marta Hoffmann notes that there is a picture of a stained glass window in the Kaiser Freidrich Museum in Berlin, dated to about 1450, that may depict a bandweaving loom with fixed heddles, but she says that the details are unclear.[47]

Another version of this loom, which uses an auxiliary bandgrind operated by a foot treadle, was used specifically for pick-up weaving. This loom was sold by Husfliden shops in Norway and in Sweden it was known as the *Leksandsbandstol* (band loom from Leksand, Dalarna county, Sweden).

To avoid confusion it should be noted that the small box loom or cradle loom, used in Norway for weaving bands in a tapestry technique, is also sometimes called a bandstol.

Band Knives and Shuttles

A bandweaver needs a way to carry the weft through the sheds and beat it firmly into place. One method is to wind the weft into a small finger hank and to beat it into place either with the fingers or a wooden *bandkniv* (band knife), like the one shown in Fig. 47.

Another method is to carry the yarn on a band *skyttel* (shuttle) that, depending on its thickness, might have one edge beveled for beating the weft into place. Some band shuttles have one or both ends shaped into points for making pick-ups. The band shuttle shown in Fig. 48 has the edge for beating reinforced with metal so the warp threads won't wear grooves into the wood over time.

Bandweaving History

Tablet weaving, a technique that produces a different kind of patterned band, is thought to be much older than pick-up weaving, and there is evidence of tablet weaving in Norway from ancient times. Fragments of tablet-woven bands dating as far back as 300–500 A.D. were found in a bog at Tegle in Rogaland.[48]

When pick-up weaving came into use is not known, but in Lithuania a thousand-year-old pick-up band was discovered: "At the burial mounds of Paragaudis . . . a tenth-century gravesite was uncovered in 1973. A woman had been buried there with various bronze ornaments. On her right elbow was placed a bundle . . . wrapped and tied twice with a sash woven by the pick-up technique with the pattern ožkanagėlis. . . . It is interesting to note that many traditional sashes from the eighteenth and nineteenth centuries with this same pattern can be found in Lithuanian museums and in private collections."[49]

We don't know when pick-up weaving began in Norway, but we can look to the bandgrind for clues. Although pick-up can be done on almost any loom, in Norway the tradition is tied to the bandgrind in many districts.

Marta Hoffmann tells us that the two oldest bandgrinder found in Norway came from the site of an archaeological excavation at Bryggen, the old wharf area in Bergen in Hordaland. One is very small, with only three bars, made of horn and dated to the 1100s. The other is only a fragment, made of wood and dated to the 1200s or 1300s.[50]

Fig. 47: Band knife, made about 1810, from Hallingdal in Buskerud.
Photo: Anne-Lise Reinsfelt/Norsk Folkemuseum.

Fig. 48: Bandweaving shuttle, dated 1821, from Hjartdal in Telemark.
Photo: Anne-Lise Reinsfelt/Norsk Folkemuseum.

Fig. 49: Bandgrind, initials M J D and year 1828 painted on front.
Photo: Vesterheim (1979.27.1).

Fig. 50: Bandgrind, initials GOD carved on one side. Other side shown in Fig. 51. *Photo: Vesterheim (Luther College Collection 1401).*

Fig. 51: Bandgrind, ANO 1790 carved on one side. Other side shown in Fig. 50. *Photo: Vesterheim (Luther College Collection 1401).*

According to Hoffmann, there are three older bandgrinder found elsewhere in Europe that apparently date back to Roman times. One found in England has bars of bone fastened to a bronze frame. Another found in Pompeii is made completely of bone. And one found in Hungary is made of bronze. All are less than 4" high and because they are fragments, their original width is unknown.[51]

The excavation of the Oseberg archaeological find, a Viking queen's burial mound in Vestfold that has been dated to 834 A.D., contained many textile tools and evidence of tablet weaving but no bandgrinder. In Iceland, which was settled by Norsemen during the Viking Age, there was no tradition of weaving on the bandgrind. Hoffmann concludes that if the bandgrind had been known in Norway during the Viking Age (793–1066 A.D.) when Iceland was settled, some evidence of it should have survived to the present.[52]

According to Inger Lise Christie, there are finely patterned and technically advanced pick-up bands in existence that are presumed to date to the 1700s, which indicates that the bandgrind was probably well-established by that time. There are some preserved bandgrinder dated to the 1600s and many more dated to the 1700s and early 1800s. Christie notes that this increase may simply be because there are more everyday items of all kinds preserved from the 1700s and later, or it may be because the bandgrind gained popularity then. She adds that the increased number of bandgrinder also corresponds to fewer examples of tablet weaving, so tablet weaving may have declined as pick-up weaving with bandgrinder became more popular.[53]

Torbjørg Gauslaa concluded that some pick-up bands from Nord-Østerdalen dated to the 1800s could have been woven using tablets.[54] Although tablet weaving was usually used to create bands in the woven structures unique to that technique, it could be used as a simple shedding mechanism to weave plain warp-faced bands or pick-up. If the tablets are turned once forward and once back so no twist forms in the warp it is impossible to tell whether a band was made with tablets or with another kind of loom.

Gauslaa arrived at her theory because many Nord-Østerdalen bands do not appear to have been woven in a bandgrind. The bandgrind spreads a warp out wider than the band being woven, and threads at the edges of bands with many warp threads tend to pull closer together than those in the middle. Many Nord-Østerdalen bands have a large number of warp threads but the threads are evenly distributed. The bandstol does not appear to have been known in Nord-Østerdalen and no other band loom capable of such fine work has survived in that area.[55] However, it is possible that such bands were woven on a large floor loom such as was used for weaving wider cloth.

In the end, all we know for sure is that pick-up weaving was well-established in Norway, at least in some areas, by the late 1600s.

Fig. 52: *Bandgrind* (band heddle) with acanthus carved decoration. *Photo: Vesterheim (Luther College Collection 1404).*

Part 2
Vesterheim Collection

The textile collection of Vesterheim Norwegian-American Museum in Decorah, Iowa (see sidebar, page 87) includes pick-up bands from many regions in Norway. According to Chief Curator Laurann Gilbertson, there were three categories of things brought by immigrants—items for the voyage, items for the new home, and items too important to leave behind. She says that bands usually fall into the last category.[1]

In this **Part** we'll look at some of the bands in the collection. We know a little about one immigrant, Barbro Ramseth, and her bands represent the two different pick-up weaves found in Norway, so we'll begin with them.

Barbro Ramseth (1838–1913) was born in Tynset in Nord-Østerdalen and immigrated to Wisconsin in 1888, with her husband and five children.[2] Her bands might have been woven during the couple's engagement, at least twenty years before they emigrated. The initials PRBID, woven in pick-up on one band, stand for Poul Ramseth (her husband) and Barbro Iversdatter (her maiden name).

Her first year in America, Barbro wrote to her father in Norway: "I often think of Tynset, and of you, then I long for home, but now, thank goodness, things are much better. I am fully convinced that it was best for us to come over here, for our experience shows that it is easier to earn money here, and fight our way through, but it is a painful process, many losses for a newcomer. The trip itself is a great hardship, but all things pass. People have been very kind to us."[3]

Both pick-up-woven bands made the long and difficult journey with the family and were saved and handed down through three more generations. In 1977, they were donated to Vesterheim by Barbro's great-grandson when they were over a hundred years old. Their history clearly shows the significance such bands had for the families who owned them.

Let's take a closer look at Barbro's bands and others from Nord-Østerdalen, Telemark, Aust-Agder, Hordaland, Sogn og Fjordane, Trøndelag, and Buskerud. Then, at the end of this **Part**, we'll look at what they can tell us about traditional colors, materials, and patterns.

Fig. 53: Band 1, bed band.
Photo: Vesterheim (1977.93.2).

Nord-Østerdalen

BAND 1

Pattern warp: Z-twist red and green wool, presumably handspun
Borders: Black wool
Background warp and weft: Natural cotton
Dimensions: 1" wide, 51" long including handle

This *sengeband* (bed band) was woven by Barbro Ramseth (1838–1913) in Tynset, Nord-Østerdalen. A bed band is a kind of handle that was common in the old days to help the old and infirm turn or get out of bed. One end of the band was tied around a ceiling beam and the other end hung down where it could be easily reached. The band is folded into a double thickness, with the fold at the top and the two layers separating to form two sides of a triangle at the bottom. A wooden rod, covered with a separate length of band, forms the bottom of the triangle and provides a solid handle. The two layers are stitched together in three places, and decorated at those points with ring-shaped tassels. The tassels are made by wrapping red wool around a bundle of yarn strands, then bending the wrapped portion into a curve and letting the yarn strands from both ends form fringe at the bottom of the ring. Although the band is worn and the wool is missing in places we can still see the initials PRBID (for Poul Ramseth and Barbro Iversdatter) woven in pick-up just above the handle.

Fig. 54: Band 2, swaddling band.
Photo: Vesterheim (1977.93.1).

Nord-Østerdalen

BAND 2

PATTERN WARP: Z-twist dark red wool, presumably handspun, natural cotton
BORDERS: Gold cotton, red wool
WEFT: Natural cotton
DIMENSIONS: 1¼" wide, 118" long

Like Band 1, this band was woven by Barbro Ramseth (1838–1913) in
Tynset, Nord-Østerdalen. According to Helga Reidun Bergebakken Nesset
of Nordøsterdalsmuseet in Tynset, this was a swaddling band.[4] It is worn
and frayed, and the wool has completely disintegrated in several places. Both
of Barbro's bands used cotton instead of linen along with the wool, which
indicates they would have been woven in the 1850s or later, since cotton yarn
came into use in Nord-Østerdalen in the 1850s.[5]

Fig: 55: Detail Band 2, swaddling band.
Photo: Vesterheim (1977.93.1).

Fig. 56: At left, Band 4, at right, Band 3.
Photo: Vesterheim (1967.37.389 and 1967.37.388).

Fig. 57: Detail, Band 4.
Photo: Vesterheim (1967.37.389).

Nord-Østerdalen

BAND 3 *(at right in top photo)*
Pattern warp: Z-twist light red wool, presumably handspun and vegetable-dyed
Borders: Light purplish-red wool, presumably handspun and vegetable-dyed
Background warp and weft: Natural linen
Dimensions: ⅝" wide, 79" long

BAND 4 *(at left in top photo)*
Pattern warp: Z-twist red wool, presumably handspun and vegetable-dyed
Borders: Red wool
Background warp and weft: Natural cotton
Dimensions: ⅝" wide, 90½" long

These bands came from Os in Nord-Østerdalen with Elias Hansen Narjord
(born in 1829) and his wife, Anne Kristine Tørrisdatter Dalen (born in
1831). The couple married in 1854, emigrated from Norway a month later,
and settled in Iowa. The bands came to Vesterheim from the estate of the
couple's only grandchild more than a hundred years later. Band 3 is woven
in a diamond and X pattern for a few inches at each end, with a zigzag
pattern along the rest of its length. Band 4 contains eight different pick-up
patterns along its length. It uses a threading that gives a whipstitched look
to the selvedges, similar to that used in Bands 1 and 2, and also common
in other districts. In both bands the fringe has been augmented by poking a
small bundle of wool strands through the center of the end of the band and
wrapping the fringe with linen for a tassel effect. According to Helga Reidun
Bergebakken Nesset of Nordøsterdalsmuseet in Tynset, these bands could have
been used as *bløyeband*. A *bløyeband* was used to hold a fine, white cloth called
the *bløye* in place as the outermost layer around a swaddled baby, as shown in
Fig. 22, **Part 1**.[6]

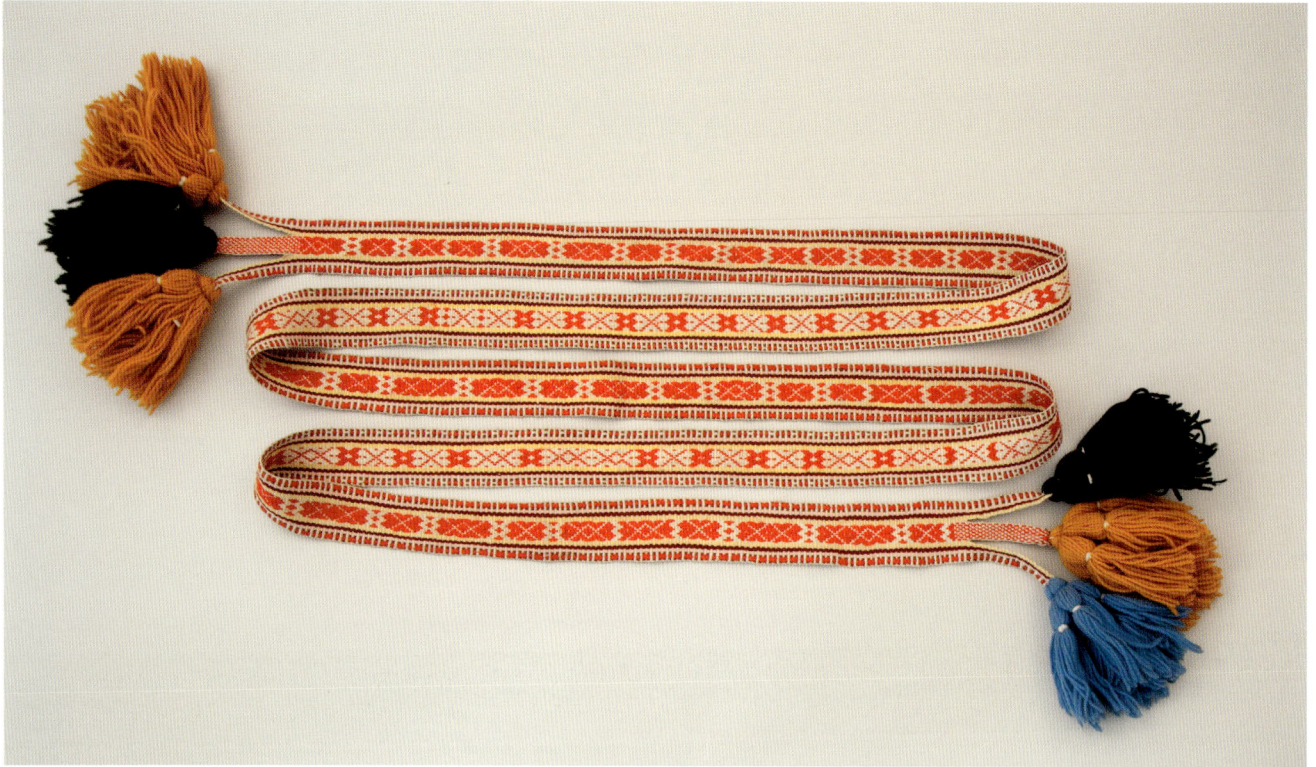

Fig. 58: Band 5, apron band.
Photo: Vesterheim (Luther College Collection 4313).

Fig. 59: Detail of Band 5, apron band.
Photo: Vesterheim (Luther College Collection 4313).

Øst-Telemark

BAND 5

Pattern warp: Red wool

Borders: Red, yellow, pink, burgundy, and brown wool

Background warp and weft: Natural cotton

Dimensions: 1¼" wide, 103" long

This band is part of Vesterheim's Luther College collection. It is finished with tabs and tassels, typical of apron bands in Øst-Telemark. The tabs are created by weaving the ends in three separate sections for a few inches. For each tassel a bundle of wool strands is cut, about twice as long as the tassel will be. The strands are laid all around the tab and parallel to it, then the middle of the bundle is tightly wrapped and stitched to the tab. Finally, the upper ends of the bundle are folded down and the whole bundle is tied together in several places. Often one tassel is in a color that contrasts with the rest, as in this band.

Fig. 60: Band 6, apron band, Band 7, hair circlet.
Photo: Vesterheim (1971.13.1).

Øst-Telemark

BANDS 6 and 7

PATTERN WARP: Red wool
BORDERS OF APRON BAND: Red, green, and yellow wool
BORDERS OF HAIRBAND: Green, yellow, and black wool
BACKGROUND WARP AND WEFT: Natural cotton
DIMENSIONS OF APRON BAND: ⅞" wide, 108" long
DIMENSIONS OF HAIRBAND: ⅞" wide, 102" long

This apron band and hairband are part of a traditional dress worn around 1875 by Anne Jonsdatter Gutukjær (1834–1915), for her second marriage, to Halvor Hansson Torstveit in Bø, Øst-Telemark. In 1887 the couple and their children immigrated to the Dakota Territory. The apron band, which has three tabs and tassels at each end, is worn under a wide, tablet-woven belt with the ends hanging down in front. The hairband, which has two tabs and tassels at each end, has been wrapped around a core to form a circlet so it can be displayed with the rest of the costume. The circlet is about 7½" in diameter, and the two ends hang down as streamers, each about 16" long.

Fig. 61: Øst-Telemark dress.
Photo: Vesterheim (1971.13.1).

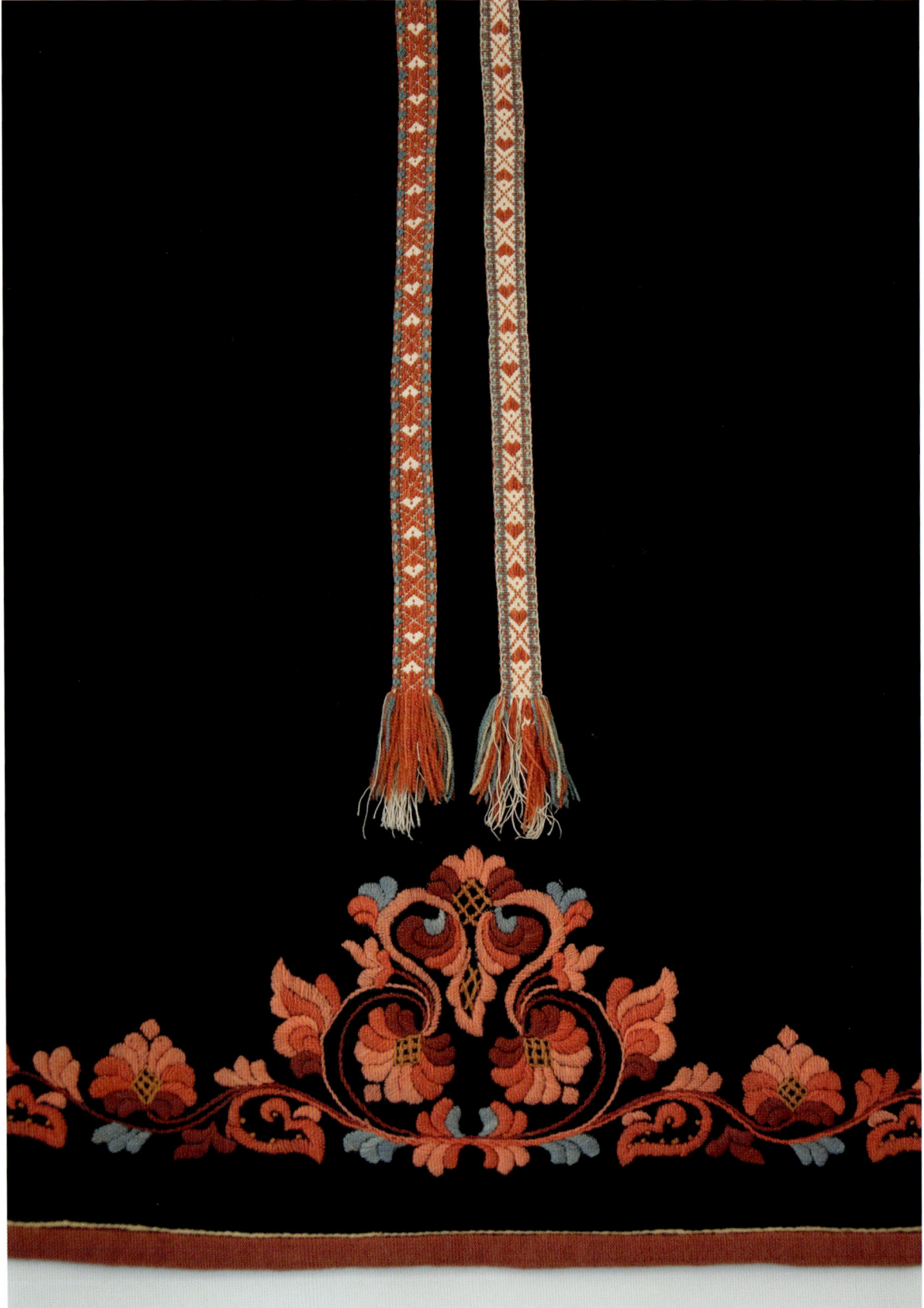

Fig. 62: Band 8, apron band.
Photo: Vesterheim (1978.68.1).

Vest-Telemark

BAND 8

PATTERN WARP: Rust-red wool
BORDERS: Rust-red, teal blue, and yellow-green wool
BACKGROUND WARP AND WEFT: Natural cotton
DIMENSIONS: ⅝" wide, 110" long

Pick-up-woven apron bands have been a part of the folk costume tradition in Vest-Telemark at least since the late 1600s and were traditionally used for church wear. This apron is part of a bunad from the early 20th century, a time when the folk costume in Vest-Telemark was being replaced with town wear and the folk costume was taking on a new role as a bunad for festive occasions. The band is attached to the waistband of the embroidered, black wool apron, and when worn it is taken twice around the waist and knotted in front. Apron bands from Vest-Telemark are typically narrower than those from Øst-Telemark.

Fig. 63: Band 9, apron band.
Photo: Vesterheim (1989.67.1).

Vest-Telemark

BANDS 9 and 10

PATTERN WARP: Red wool

BORDERS: Red, green, and yellow wool

BACKGROUND WARP AND WEFT: Natural cotton

DIMENSIONS OF APRON BAND: ¾" wide, 103" long

DIMENSIONS OF HAIRBAND: ¾" wide, wrapped around core to form circlet approx. 7½" in diameter, with two streamers each approx. 16" long

This apron band and hair circlet are part of a Vest-Telemark bunad from the mid-20th century. The apron band is attached to the waistband of the embroidered wool apron, and when worn it is taken twice around the waist and knotted in front. The hair circlet is used by women whose hair is not long enough to braid with a band in the traditional fashion. Such circlets are made by wrapping the band around a roll of felt, bundle of combed flax, or hank of real hair, and forming it into a wreath shape that is worn on the crown of the head with the ends of the band hanging down as streamers.

Fig. 64: Band 10, hair circlet.
Photo: Vesterheim (1989.67.1).

Fig. 65: Band 11, belt, and Band 12, hairband.
Photo: Vesterheim (1997.63.1).

Setesdal in Aust-Agder

BANDS 11 and 12

PATTERN WARP: Red and green wool
BORDERS: Red and green wool pick-up pattern, pink and green wool stripes
BACKGROUND WARP AND WEFT: Natural linen
DIMENSIONS OF BELT: 2" wide, 100" long
DIMENSIONS OF HAIRBAND: 1" wide, 105" long

This belt and hairband are part of a folk costume worn by a descendant of Guy Kjoivestad, who emigrated from Valle in Setesdal. In Setesdal in Aust-Agder, pick-up weaving was used for the best belts and hairbands, those intended for church wear. For everyday, women wore hairbands made in simpler weaving techniques and a leather belt instead of the woven one. The belt is mitered and stitched to a silver clasp, with enough length between the two halves of the clasp so it can be wrapped twice around the waist. When worn, the clasp is fastened at the side front and the two ends with long fringe hang down over the skirt.

Setesdal bands use a threading variation that creates diagonal pattern lines that are less steep than usual. Stripes in pink, red, and green separate the border patterns from the main patterns. The two most common main patterns in Setesdal are *kross og kringle* (diagonal cross and diamond shape) and *krok* (crooked line or zigzag). Kross og kringle is also called the swaddling weave, since swaddling bands were woven in that pattern, as shown in Fig. 20, **Part 1**. The most common belt pattern is the krok. Here the zigzag is recessed in white background color on the front of the band, with the red pattern color forming a raised pattern around it. The hairband uses the same pattern as the belt but in a narrower version.

Fig. 66: Setesdal dress.
Photo: Vesterheim (1997.63.1).

Fig. 67: Band 13, belt.
Photo: Vesterheim (2003.42.2).

Åmli in Aust-Agder

BAND 13

PATTERN WARP: Red wool
BORDERS: Red, green, yellow, and black wool
BACKGROUND WARP AND WEFT: Natural linen
DIMENSIONS: 1" wide, 74" long

This belt is part of a bunad made in Norway in 1967 for Grace Nelson Rikansrud of Decorah, Iowa. Åmli, like Setesdal, is in Aust-Agder, but the costumes from the two districts are very different. The Åmli belt does not use the Setesdal threading variation, and the borders are woven plain, without a pick-up pattern, in stripes and alternating horizontal bars. The belt is half as wide as the Setesdal belt and is wrapped only once around the waist. At each end 3" is woven plain, without pick-ups, showing the staggered flecks that this threading produces in plain weave. The belt is mitered and stitched to the holes in the heart-shaped silver buckle, which fastens with a hook-and-eye closure. When worn, about 20" of each fringed end hangs down in front. The diagonal cross pattern in this belt is one of five pick-up patterns that can be chosen for the Åmli bunad.

Fig. 68: Åmli bunad.
Photo: Vesterheim (2003.42.2).

Fig. 69: At left, Band 14, one of pair of belt hangings,
at right, Band 15, belt.
Photo: Vesterheim (1974.6.3 and 1976.83.19).

Hardanger in Hordaland

BAND 14 *(at left in photo)*
PATTERN WARP: Red and green wool
BORDERS: Yellow, green, red, and blue wool
BACKGROUND WARP AND WEFT: Natural linen
DIMENSIONS: Two pieces, each 2" wide and 32" long
FINISH: Ends bound in green velvet fabric

BAND 15 *(at right in photo)*
PATTERN WARP: Red and green wool
BORDERS: Yellow, green, red, and blue wool
BACKGROUND WARP AND WEFT: Natural linen
DIMENSIONS: 2" wide and 33" long
FINISH: Ends bound in black velvet fabric

Both of these bands were woven in Hardanger, and Band 15 was brought from Hardanger in 1880. In the Hardanger region of Hordaland, pick-up was one technique used to make belts and *fangband* (lap bands or belt hangings) for the woman's costume. Some costumes used belts and hangings made with embroidery or leather decorated with silver instead. The belt was fastened around the waist and two lap bands were attached so they hung down from the belt as decoration on the outside of the apron, one on each side of center. In some districts of Hardanger the belt hangings were worn only by married women. In other districts they were also worn by unmarried girls. Band 14 is part of a set of two, presumably lap bands. Band 15 is presumably a belt. The motifs used in Hardanger are similar to those used in Telemark, and the borders are also similar in that they are woven in a different pick-up technique from the main pattern section. But the Hardanger bands are much wider and the main pattern section is set off from the pick-up borders with stripes.

Fig. 70: Band 16, coat band.
Photo: Vesterheim (2000.11.1).

Hordaland

BAND 16

Pattern warp: Red wool

Borders: Red and black wool

Background warp and weft: Natural cotton

Dimensions: 1¼" wide, 138" long

Finish: Bound on the ends with red wool and brown velvet

This band came from Norway with Marthinus Wilhemson Østreim, who was born in 1857 and emigrated in 1872 from Austrheim, then a part of Lindås parish, in northern Hordaland. His family in Minnesota remembered how he used this band to tie shut a big buttonless cloak that he wore, showing that some immigrants continued to wear traditional garments in America. The band is finished on the ends in the same manner as some christening bands, so perhaps it originally served that purpose before being converted to use as a coat band. Coat bands and swaddling bands actually serve related purposes and can be of similar length. In both cases, a long band is wrapped around the body, often with a cross over the chest, to hold clothing closely in place for warmth.

Fig. 71: Band 17, swaddling band.
Photo: Vesterheim (1986.133.1).

Sogn og Fjordane

BAND 17

Pattern warp: Red and dark blue wool, natural cotton
Weft: Natural cotton
Dimensions: 1½" wide, 138" long

This band was donated to Vesterheim in 1986 by the daughter of author Ole Rølvaag and is believed to have come from Sogn og Fjordane where some ancestors of her family lived. Its dimensions and style indicate that it was likely a swaddling band.

Fig. 72: Band 18.
Photo: Vesterheim (1984.35.6).

Sogn og Fjordane

BAND 18

Pᴀᴛᴛᴇʀɴ ᴡᴀʀᴘ: Red wool

Bᴀᴄᴋɢʀᴏᴜɴᴅ ᴡᴀʀᴘ ᴀɴᴅ ᴡᴇꜰᴛ: Natural cotton

Dɪᴍᴇɴꜱɪᴏɴꜱ: ½" wide, 86" long

This band was brought from Sogn og Fjordane in 1867 by the donor's grandfather and grandmother, Ola Nilsson Vangsness and Anne Johannesdatter Fidkje. In a letter to Vesterheim the donor said, "As far as I know, such bands were woven especially to hold the wraps on youngsters. This was before safety pins were invented."[7] The dimensions of this band are not those of a swaddling band but perhaps it was used as a *bløyeband*, to hold a fine, white cloth called the *bløye* in place as the outermost layer around a swaddled baby. Bands from Sogn og Fjordane and other areas north of Hordaland and Telemark were woven with no border pattern at all, as in this band, or with a simple border of narrow stripes or bars. They did not use the pick-up borders seen in Telemark bands.

Fig. 73: Band 19, stocking band, one of pair.
Photo: Vesterheim (2003.36.9).

Trøndelag

BAND 19

Pattern warp: Red and orange wool
Borders: Blue and red wool
Background warp and weft: Natural cotton
Dimensions: Set of two, each ⅝" wide, 47" long

These stocking bands were brought from Trøndelag by Ludvig Marrinius Opøien (later Louis M. Larson) when he emigrated in 1887 at the age of 23. The band pictured is one of a pair. Stocking bands were woven in a single strip that was cut apart in the middle to form the pair, each band with fringe at only one end. The fringe was often augmented with additional yarn to form a kind of tassel, as seen here. Men wore stocking bands with knee-length breeches, wrapping them around the top of the stocking below the knee and letting the fringed ends hang down. These particular stocking bands alternate two colors of red in the pattern for an interesting effect.

Fig. 74: Band 20, suspenders for skirt.
Photo: Vesterheim (2001.41.1).

Øvre-Numedal in Buskerud

BAND 20

Pattern warp: Red and violet wool
Borders: Violet, gold, and yellow wool
Background warp and weft: Natural cotton
Dimensions: 1" wide

These suspenders are part of a folk costume, brought from Norway in 1938, that is believed to date from around 1850. It belonged to Helvig Braafladt and might have served as her wedding costume. The traditional dress for festive occasions in Øvre-Numedal, called the *skjælingskleda*, was no longer commonly used by 1900, but there were preserved examples that served as models for bunader. The suspenders are attached to the black wool skirt and when worn are visible in the back between the skirt and the short jacket.

Two Pick-up Weaves

Barbro Ramseth's bands represent the two different pick-up weaves found in Norway. The bed band (Band 1) is what in Nord-Østerdalen would be called *mønsterband* (pattern band) and the swaddling band (Band 2) is what in Nord-Østerdalen would be called *parband* (pair band). Each weave requires a different threading, different weaving techniques, and yields different kinds of patterns, as fully explained in **Part 3**, where parband and mønsterband are referred to as Type 1 pick-up and Type 2 pick-up respectively.

In the weave used for the bed band (Band 1), colored motifs have a raised or embossed appearance, with a light background that recedes around them in a basketweave texture. In the weave used for the swaddling band (Band 2), patterns are formed by a network of interlocking floats in two colors, and the network often covers the entire surface of the band. The floats are picked up in pairs, thus the name parband.

The weave in Band 2 is the less common of the two. It is used for borders in Bands 5, 6, 8, 9, 10, 11, 12, 14, and 15, from Telemark, Setesdal, and Hardanger, and as a border technique it provides an interesting contrast to the main pattern. In addition to Band 2, Band 17 from Sogn og Fjordane is woven entirely in this weave.

The remaining bands shown here use the same weave as Band 1, either for the main pattern section or the entire band. This weave looks good on both the back and front, as you can see in the photos of Bands 3–10, 14, 15, 18, 19, and 20. The side with the predominance of pattern color is usually considered the right side, but on the back the pattern and background colors change places and create equally pleasing designs. In the less common weave, the floats are all on the front, but a white shadow of the pattern appears in the weave texture on the back, as you can see in the photo of Band 2.

Traditional Materials and Colors

In the oldest Norwegian bands, natural linen was used for the background, and handspun, vegetable-dyed *spelsaugarn* (yarn from the spelsau, a Norwegian breed of sheep) was used for the pattern. Most handspun yarns were two-ply.

Those who had the means could purchase imported, factory-made wool yarn to use instead of handspun. In Vest-Telemark, Aagot Noss found a belt listed in a probate record from 1759 as a *Flandergarnsbelte* (Flanders yarn belt), which she says presumably meant that the yarn was imported from Flanders.[8] In Setesdal, the imported wool yarn that was used for embroidery on folk costumes gradually replaced handspun, vegetable-dyed wool for pick-up belts. The bands in Vesterheim's collection were woven in a variety of wools, from sturdy handspuns to soft, springy wools like those spun commercially for handknitting.

As cotton yarn became available in the 1800s, it gradually replaced linen for the background in many bands. According to Torbjørg Gauslaa, it was common for women to buy a singles cotton and then ply two, three, four, or even six strands together on the spinning wheel.[9] Many of Vesterheim's bands have a natural cotton background of various plies and the yarn might have been made in this way.

Gauslaa noted that band patterns had a more lively appearance when the twist in the cotton or linen background yarn and the wool pattern yarn were opposite—S-twist in one and Z-twist in the other.[10] We can see this effect in Bands 1, 3, and 4 from Nord-Østerdalen.

Red was by far the most common color for the main pattern. Madder root was a very important red dyestuff and was being imported into Norway by the early 1800s. It could be used to obtain several shades of red. A lichen dye known as *korkje*, which had been known in Norway for hundreds of years, was used to obtain a red-violet color. The light, purplish-red in Band 3 from Nord-Østerdalen might have come from korkje. The roots of broomstraw were also used to obtain several shades of red.

When aniline dyes came into use around 1870, sharper, brighter colors replaced the softer hues of vegetable dyes. At that time, belts with pink pattern yarn instead of red were fashionable in Setesdal for a time, and pink belts were also seen around WWI, when red yarn was difficult to get. Although not used for the pattern color, we can see pink in the border stripes in Bands 11 and 12 from Setesdal.

Norwegian bands often have several pattern threads in a different color, usually in the center of the band. This not only provides an interesting accent, but helps the weaver keep track of her place as she picks up the threads. You can see this effect in Band 1, where green is used for the three center pattern threads.

Pattern Motifs

Pattern charts made from Bands 1–20 are shown in Figs. 76–83. Also included are two charts made from Telemark bands not photographed, Vesterheim 1994.28.3, and Vesterheim 1986.93.24. The charts are drawn on a square grid but patterns usually appear more elongated in the woven bands.

Some motifs are common, appearing in different forms in many districts. **Zigzags** are one example, as in Bands 3 and 4 from Nord-Østerdalen, and Bands 11 and 12 from Setesdal. **Diamonds and Xs** (lozenges alternating with diagonal crosses) are another example, as in Band 3 (at the ends) and Band 4 (in one section), both from Nord-Østerdalen, Band 13 from Åmli, and Band 19 from Trøndelag. The **doubled cross** alternating with the **diamond scored with a cross** is a third example, as in Bands 14 and 16 from Hordaland. I refer to these as hatched motifs and they also appear in various forms in Telemark and Nord-Østerdalen.

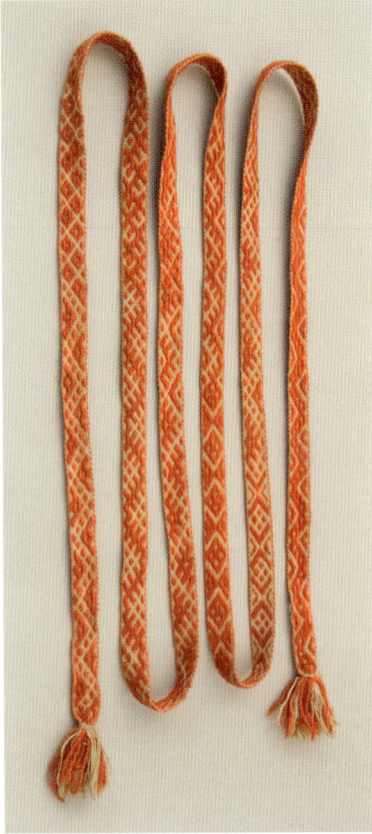

Fig. 75: Band 4.
Photo: Vesterheim (1967.37.389).

In Telemark, the **rosette** is a common motif. Band 5 uses a basic rosette and several modified and elongated versions. When the rosette is extended at both ends to form a kind of combination **rosette-cross**, and then alternated with a simple diagonal cross, a **heart** in background color appears between the motifs, as in Bands 6 and 8. When the rosette-cross is repeated without the alternating simple cross, diamond shapes appear in background color between the motifs, as in Band 7. The basic rosette can also be modified to a more defined **eight-petaled rose**. Sometimes the rose is woven in pattern color, as in Band 10, and sometimes it appears in background color between rosette-crosses, as in Band 9. Various forms of the rosette are also used in other districts, as in Band 15 from Hordaland.

Two Vesterheim bands not photographed here are included in Fig. 83. They illustrate other typical Telemark patterns—rosette-crosses alternating with hatched crosses and hatched diamonds (Vesterheim 1994.28.3) and diagonal crosses alternating with crosswise zigzag lines (Vesterheim 1986.93.24).

In Øvre-Numedal in Buskerud many of the patterns are similar to those from Telemark, but the borders are in simple stripes and bars, as opposed to the contrasting pick-up borders used in most Telemark bands. Apron bands from Øvre-Numedal are patterned with diamonds and Xs, hatched patterns and rosette variations, while the skirt suspenders use a distinctive variation of the eight-petaled rose, as in Band 20.

In Nord-Østerdalen, continuous patterns, like those in Band 4, are common. These often have an even distribution of pattern color and background color, rather than a predominance of pattern color on the right side. Notice the hatched diamond patterns that appear in background color between the toothed diagonal lines in Band 4. Patterns formed by two alternating motifs are also used in Nord-Østerdalen, as in Band 1, and the solid triangle shape there is characteristic of Nord-Østerdalen. Band 18 from Sogn og Fjordane is an example of a continuous pattern from another district.

A Brief History of
Vesterheim Norwegian-American Museum

Now numbering 24,000 objects, the collection started in 1877 as a study aid for students at Luther College in Decorah, Iowa. The first gift to the museum was a collection of birds' eggs and nests. In the early years, the collection included natural history (biology, geology) and cultural items, some of which had been collected by Lutheran missionaries serving around the globe.

By 1895, faculty and alumni at Luther College officially resolved that Norwegian immigrant materials should be a stated focus of the collection. In doing so, the museum became a pioneer in the preservation and promotion of America's cultural diversity. The museum became a natural repository for items that might otherwise have been thrown away.

The first historic building was added to the grounds in 1913, starting the Open Air Division. No other museum in the United States was collecting buildings, though this was already taking place in Scandinavia. Skansen, in Stockholm, Sweden, and Norsk Folkemuseum in Oslo, Norway, were the world's first open-air museums.

In 1925, in honor of 100 years of emigration, Anders Sandvig (founder of Maihaugen in Lillehammer, Norway) coordinated a gift of artifacts from Norwegian museums. "May these objects work," wrote Sandvig, "so that the Norwegian-ness in you will not die too soon, and the connection with the homeland will because of this be tighter. Receive this gift as proof that we follow you all in our hearts, even though the big Atlantic parts us." The gift took two years to assemble and filled 23 crates. The museum in Nordmøre sent several clothing items including two men's shirts trimmed with fine whitework embroidery. They would have no way of knowing that this gift meant the survival of several cultural treasures because their museum would be destroyed during World War II.

After the war, director Inga Bredesen Norstog created a national audience through articles in newspapers and magazines. Soon the museum was receiving visitors and artifact donations from all over the United States.

The museum became an independent institution in 1964 and adopted the name Vesterheim in honor of the term that immigrants used to describe America in letters home. America was their vesterheim, their western home.

Beginning in the 1960s, director Marion Nelson showed visitors that there was art in everyday objects and added fine art to the museum's collection statement. Today? We are "refining" the collection—looking to fill gaps to ensure that Vesterheim's artifacts can tell more stories of immigrant experiences, of American experiences.

Laurann Gilbertson
Chief Curator
Vesterheim Norwegian-American Museum

Fig. 76: Left to right, charts of
Vesterheim Bands 1, 2, and 3.

Fig. 77: Charts of Vesterheim Band 4.

Fig. 78: Charts of Vesterheim Band 4.

Fig. 79: At left, four charts of Vesterheim
Band 5. At right, chart of pattern used in
Vesterheim Bands 6 and 8.

Fig. 80: Left to right, charts of
Vesterheim Bands 7, 9, 10, and 11.

Fig. 81: Left to right, charts of
Vesterheim Bands 12, 13, 14, and 15.

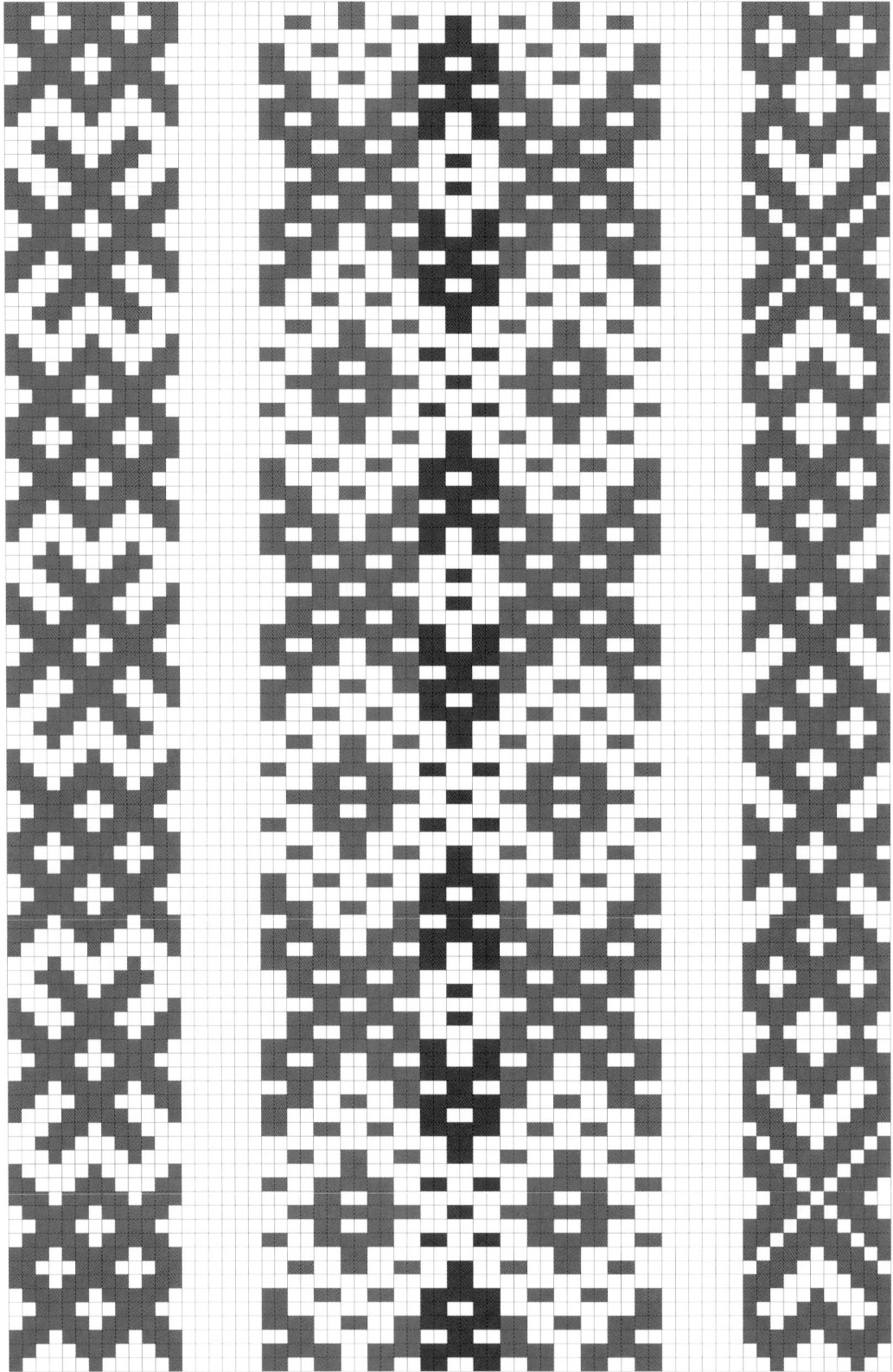

Fig. 82: Left to right, charts of
Vesterheim Bands 16, 17, and 18.

Fig. 83: Left to right, charts of Vesterheim Bands 19 and 20, Vesterheim 1994.28.3, and Vesterheim 1986.93.24.

Part 3

How to Weave Pick-up

Pick-up weaving is full of fascinating design possibilities. From a simple threading you can "pluck forth" hundreds of intricate and colorful patterns, watching them blossom row by row, varying them endlessly. The process of weaving—changing sheds, beating, and passing the shuttle back and forth—creates a pleasant, relaxing rhythm. And as you make the pick-ups, you feel intimately connected with the threads you hold in your hands and the patterns that unfold as you work.

Pick-up creates intricate patterns, but it's not difficult to do. There are just a few simple motions to learn and these are clearly illustrated in the instructions that follow. Charts tell you everything you need to know to weave specific patterns, and once you understand the basics you'll see that it's easy to modify charts or create your own. Because a pick-up pattern is an integral part of the weave structure and grows naturally out of the threading, the process of weaving pick-up will soon feel natural too.

Fig: 84: The *bandgrind* (band heddle) is portable and easy to use, and the patterns are fun to weave. Here my dog, Peter, checks out the reversible pattern from the underside.

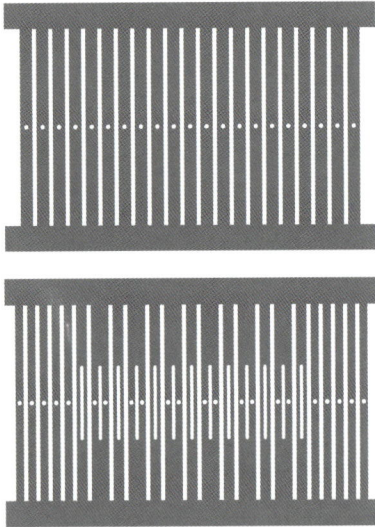

Fig. 85: **Band heddle** (top) and **pattern heddle** (bottom). The difference is that the pattern heddle has additional short slots for the pattern threads.

This **Part** covers information about tools, materials, and planning projects, as well as instructions for warping, weaving a plain band, and weaving pick-up bands with a variety of traditional Norwegian motifs. Let's get started by talking about the kind of loom you need and then defining the terms we'll use.

Looms

These instructions are written for the bandgrind and the spaltegrind, which we'll call the **band heddle** and the **pattern heddle** from now on. See Fig. 85. The band heddle is a simple and appealing tool that connect weavers with the long history of bandweaving in Norway. Its cousin, the pattern heddle, was not used in the old Norwegian farm society but is much used in Norway today. Both are easy to use, small, compact, and portable. But pick-up can also be woven on other kinds of looms.

A good, sturdy **inkle loom** is ideal because it's made specifically for weaving bands. A **floor or table loom** with two or four shafts can be used by threading for plain weave, removing the reed, and beating with the shuttle. A **rigid heddle loom**, which tensions the warp between beams in a frame, is not ideal because of the fixed distance between the heddle, where the warp is spread out, and the cloth beam, where the band is narrow. When a rigid heddle is used with a backstrap, as the band heddle is, a good distance is maintained by holding it at arm's length.

If you use an inkle or shaft loom, simply apply the pick-up instructions for the band heddle (not the pattern heddle) to the loom you already know, threading for plain weave in the color order given.

Bandweaving Terms

A woven band is created when a continuous crosswise thread, called the **weft,** is interlaced at right angles with a set of lengthwise threads of predetermined length, called the **warp**. A single warp thread is called an **end**. In other forms of weaving, a single row of weft is sometimes called a "pick," but here I call it a **row** to avoid confusion with the noun or adjective "pick-up," and the verb "to pick up."

In **warp-faced plain weave**, the weft travels over odd-numbered warp ends and under even-numbered warp ends on one row, and on the next row it does the opposite. These two rows alternate throughout. The warp is spaced closely together so the weft is visible only at the edges where it turns to weave the next row. See Fig. 86. The width of a band is determined by the number of ends in the warp, the thickness of the yarn, and how tightly the weft is pulled to draw the warp together. Warp-faced plain weave, sometimes referred to in these instructions simply as **plain weave**, forms the foundation for pick-up weaving and is also used for borders in pick-up bands.

In this band, 35 lengthwise **warp** threads, called **ends,** are visible on alternate rows.

In a warp-faced band, crosswise **weft** thread is visible only at the edges where it turns to go into the next row.

Side View

Warp end

Weft

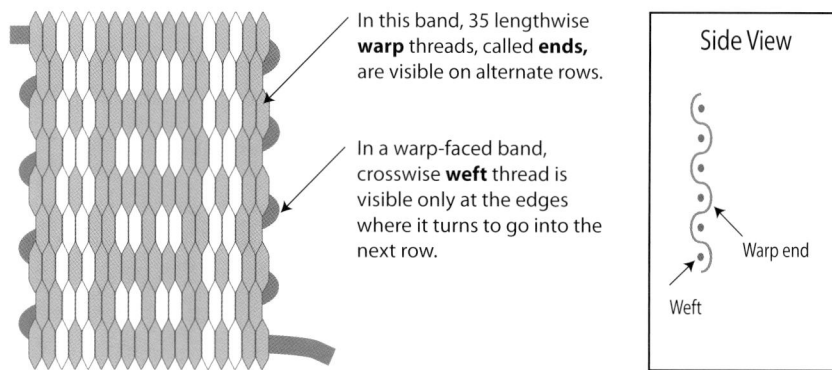

Fig. 86: Warp-faced plain weave forms the foundation for pick-up weaving and is also used for borders in many pick-up bands. Designs in warp-faced plain weave consist of simple lengthwise stripes, crosswise bars, and flecks of color created by varying the order of colors in the warp.

During weaving, the warp is held under tension on a frame or **loom**. The process of placing the warp on the loom in preparation for weaving is called **warping**. The loom has a mechanism called a **heddle** to raise and lower alternate warp ends to create the space for the weft to pass through. This space is called the **shed**. Different kinds of bandweaving looms have different heddles, but all produce the two sheds necessary for plain weave.

The **band heddle** is a hole-and-slot heddle made for weaving bands. It is part of a backstrap loom, which means that the warp is tensioned between a belt tied around the weaver's waist and a fixed point a short distance away. The warp yarn is threaded through the holes and slots, and the sheds are formed simply by moving the heddle up and down. When the heddle is pulled up, the warp ends in the slots slide to the bottom, while the warp ends in the holes form the upper level of the **up-shed**. When the heddle is pushed down, the warp ends in the slots slide to the top, while the warp ends in the holes form the lower level of the **down-shed**. See Fig. 87.

The weft is wrapped around a **shuttle** to make it easier to pass through the shed. On each row, after the shed is changed, the weft in the previous row is **beat** or packed firmly into place with the edge of the shuttle. The **fell** is the line just above the last row of weft where the beating takes place.

Pick-up Overview

Pick-up weaving is a technique for creating complex patterns on simple threadings by modifying the shed before the weft is taken through. On the band heddle, you make plain-weave sheds with the heddle and then pick up, and sometimes push down, particular **pattern ends** (ends in pattern color) on each row.

Picking up pattern ends creates floats in pattern color on the surface of the band. **Floats** combine to form **motifs** like diamonds. A **pattern** is made up of one or more motifs arranged in a certain order, together with the background effects between motifs.

There are two kinds of Norwegian pick-up, Type 1 and Type 2. In Type 1, two pattern colors alternate in the warp. The motifs can be either geometric or

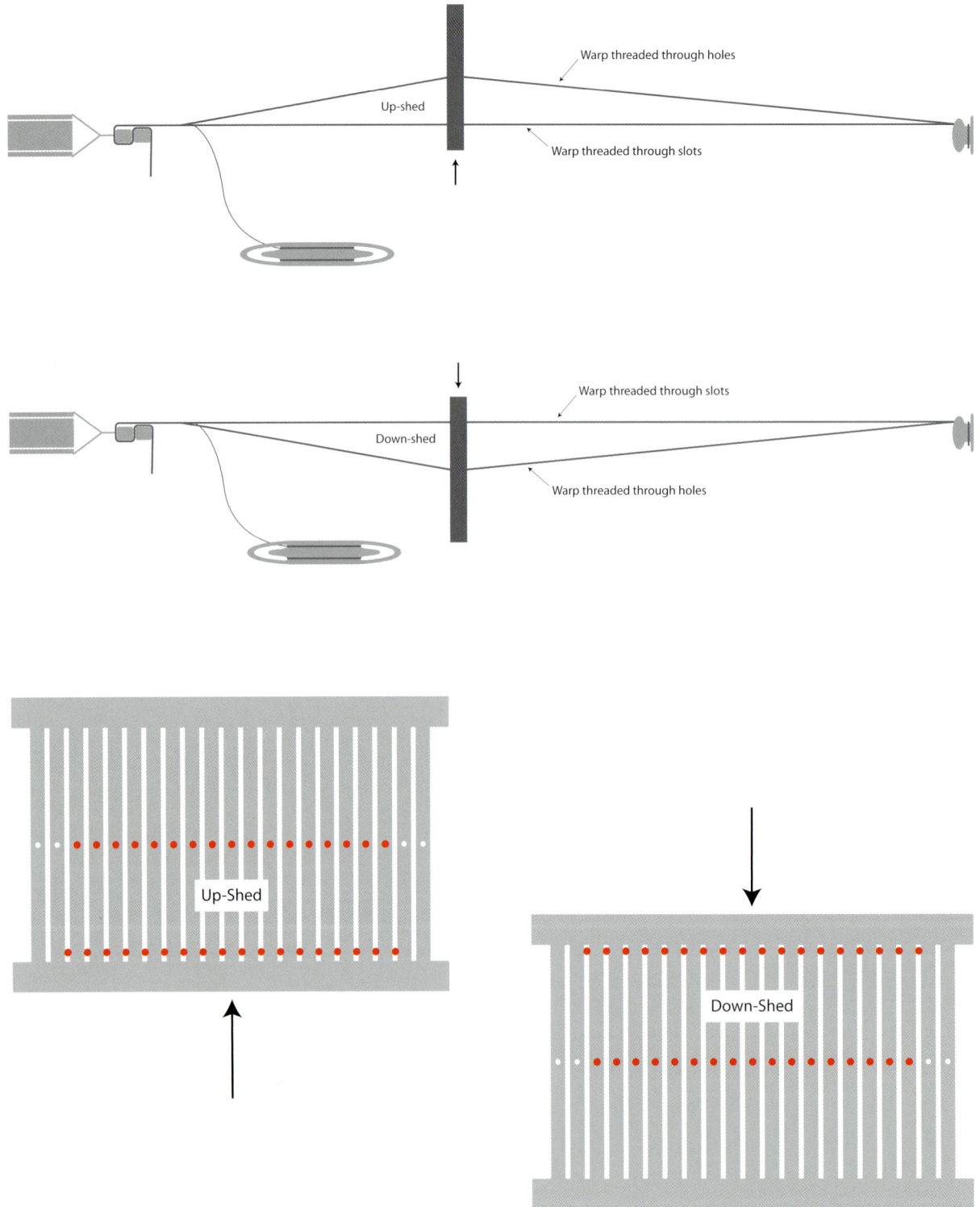

Fig. 87: **How sheds are formed on band heddle**. Warp ends (red dots) are threaded alternately through holes and slots. When the heddle is moved up, the ends in the slots slide to the bottom, and when the heddle is moved down, the ends in the slots slide to the top, forming the two sheds for weaving.

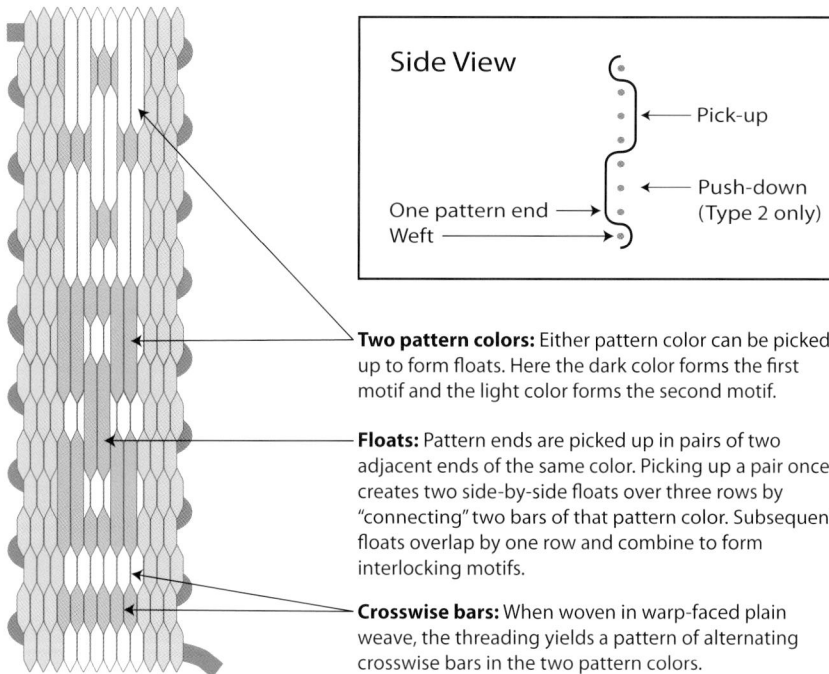

Side View

Pick-up

Push-down (Type 2 only)

One pattern end →
Weft →

Two pattern colors: Either pattern color can be picked up to form floats. Here the dark color forms the first motif and the light color forms the second motif.

Floats: Pattern ends are picked up in pairs of two adjacent ends of the same color. Picking up a pair once creates two side-by-side floats over three rows by "connecting" two bars of that pattern color. Subsequent floats overlap by one row and combine to form interlocking motifs.

Crosswise bars: When woven in warp-faced plain weave, the threading yields a pattern of alternating crosswise bars in the two pattern colors.

Type 1 Pick-up

Fig. 88: **Type 1 weave structure (upper diagram)**: In the warp, two pattern colors of the same thickness alternate throughout the pattern area. There are an even number of pattern ends (here six dark and six white) because they are picked up in pairs. **Type 2 weave structure (lower diagram)**: In the warp, pattern ends (grey) are always separated by two background ends (white) and there are always an odd number of pattern ends (seven here), so motifs can pivot on a center end. **Both types**: The more pattern ends, the more complex the patterns that can be woven. Float length is usually limited to five rows, but in some Type 2 patterns, ends are picked up three or four times in succession, for 7- or 9-row floats.

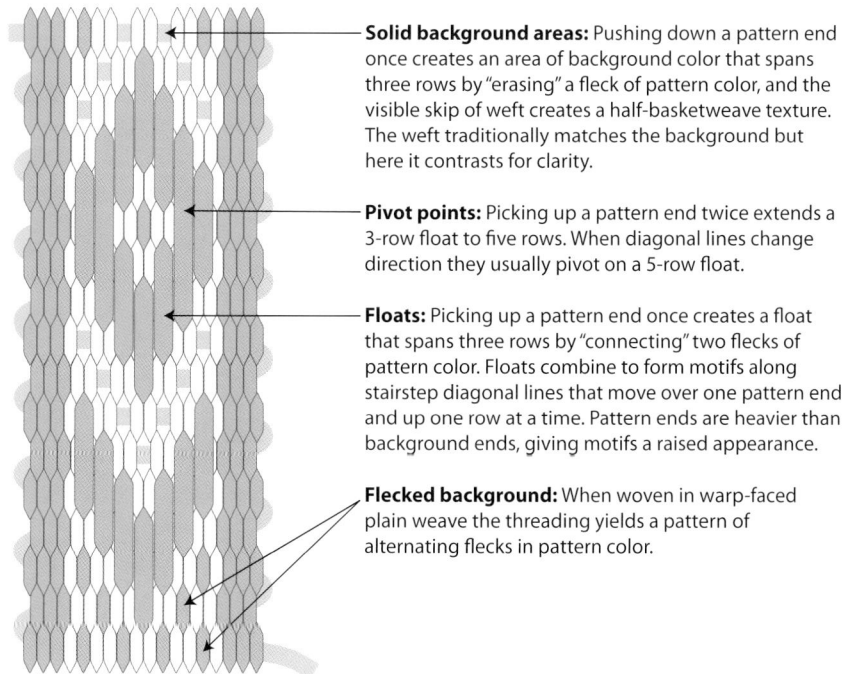

Solid background areas: Pushing down a pattern end once creates an area of background color that spans three rows by "erasing" a fleck of pattern color, and the visible skip of weft creates a half-basketweave texture. The weft traditionally matches the background but here it contrasts for clarity.

Pivot points: Picking up a pattern end twice extends a 3-row float to five rows. When diagonal lines change direction they usually pivot on a 5-row float.

Floats: Picking up a pattern end once creates a float that spans three rows by "connecting" two flecks of pattern color. Floats combine to form motifs along stairstep diagonal lines that move over one pattern end and up one row at a time. Pattern ends are heavier than background ends, giving motifs a raised appearance.

Flecked background: When woven in warp-faced plain weave the threading yields a pattern of alternating flecks in pattern color.

Type 2 Pick-up

representational and are formed by a network of interlocking floats in either or both of the pattern colors. Often the floats completely cover the surface of the band, so that motifs in one color are surrounded with a background area of floats in the other color. In Type 2, thicker ends in pattern color are always separated by two finer ends in background color. The patterns are characterized by diagonal lines, raised motifs with an embossed appearance, and a background that recedes in a half-basketweave texture around motifs. See Fig. 88 for descriptions of the two different weave structures.

The band heddle can be used to weave either kind of pick-up band. The pattern heddle has additional short slots for the ends in pattern color, and is specifically designed to weave Type 2 bands using a special patterning technique.

Where to Begin

Before you learn pick-up, you should be comfortable with warping your heddle and weaving plain-weave bands, so instructions are given first for those basic skills. If you're already familiar with the basics you can start with the pick-up instructions.

To learn the techniques for weaving pick-up, there are row-by-row instructions for making three narrow bands with simple patterns. You can choose which band to start with, depending on whether you want to weave Type 1 or Type 2 pick-up, and whether you're using the band heddle or the pattern heddle. In the Pattern Supplement at the end of this **Part**, there are patterns for more complex bands.

Norwegian Names for Pick-up

In Norway, the two pick-up weaves are sometimes referred to collectively with terms such as *mønstervevde bånd* (pattern-woven bands), *grindvevde bånd* (bands woven on the band heddle) or *bånd med opp-plukket mønster* (bands with picked-up patterns). Bands in Type 1 are sometimes referred to as *ripsbånd med plukk* (rep bands with pick-up) and bands in Type 2 are sometimes referred to as *plukkbånd* or *plukkaband* (pick-up bands). There are many regional dialects in Norway so spellings and local names vary.

In Nord-Østerdalen, bands in Type 1 are called *parband* (pair bands), those in Type 2 are called *mønsterband* (pattern bands), and the process of pick-up weaving is called *bregding*.[1] Bands from some regions, like Telemark, combine the two pick-up weaves, using Type 2 in the main pattern section and Type 1 in the borders, for an interesting contrast and distinctive appearance. In Vest-Telemark, the pick-up band is referred to as a *brogdaband* (patterned band) and is defined by how many pattern ends there are in the main pattern section. One with 9 pattern ends is called a *ni-trådsband* (9-thread band), one with 11 pattern ends is called an *elleve-trådsband* (11-thread band), and so forth. The *utbrogd* (outer pattern) is the narrow border pattern in Type 1 along the sides, usually woven in what is called the *geiteklauv* (goat's hoof) pattern. The *innbrogd* (inner pattern) is the main pattern section in Type 2 in the middle of the band. In the old days it was said that "*brogdi skulle helst vera dobbel så brei som utbrogdi* (the main pattern section should preferably be twice as wide as the border pattern)."[2]

Fig. 89: Perle cotton bands form handles that also function as closures for these knitted-and-fulled wool pouches. The small pouch handle is Type 1, and the large pouch handle is Type 2 pick-up.

What You Can Make

Pick-up is perfect for anything that requires a strong or decorative band or ribbon. For those who sew, weave, knit, and felt, pick-up makes excellent trim for aprons, hats, mittens, sweaters, vests, and blankets. The trim can be purely decorative or it can serve to reinforce or cover a raw edge. Pick-up also makes strong handles for bags and purses, and handy loops for hanging things like tools and utensils.

Bookmarks make excellent gifts and are a good way to try out many different pick-up patterns on one warp. For larger projects you can sew bands together to make wider items like pillows and purses.

If you want something traditional you might make a band for a special sending basket. If you want something modern, you might design a woven necklace, wristlet, or special lanyard. You can also use the charted patterns for another craft like knitting. In fact, Annemor Sundbø says that the border patterns in the traditional Setesdal sweater could have been derived from the pick-up patterns in the belts of the Setesdal folk costume,[3] which pre-date the sweaters.

Making a variety of bands in the colors and patterns that appeal to you is the best way to learn the techniques and you'll find lots of ways to use them once they're done. While this is not a project book, ideas for several projects are

Fig. 90: A wool and cotton band forms a hanging loop for a pewter replica of an old *primstav* (calendar stick). The pattern is from Band 18 in **Part 2**.

shown: weaving belts, loops to hold tools, pouch handles, bookmarks, journal keepers, ribbons, basket bands, and a belt to hold a knitter's *nøstekrok* (hook for holding ball of knitting yarn). The pouch handles shown in Fig. 89 are just one example of how bands can be used to trim woven, knitted, or felted items. A loop for hanging is shown in Fig. 90.

Tools and Supplies

Band heddle. You can weave both Type 1 and Type 2 pick-up on the band heddle, which comes in many shapes and sizes. The size of the holes and slots limits the size of the yarn you can use. The number of holes and slots determines the maximum number of warp ends you can have. Heddles with two rows of holes are often used for a kind of warp brocade that is beyond the scope of this book, but I use them for pick-up weaving by threading only one row of holes. The **pattern heddle** is made specifically for weaving bands in Type 2. It has separate short slots for the pattern ends and uses a different pick-up technique than the band heddle.

Pattern heddle, band heddle, or both? If you have a pattern heddle you'll also want a band heddle for weaving bands in plain weave and Type 1 pick-up. The band heddle is more versatile in that you can use it to weave plain weave, Type 1 and Type 2. But some people find it easier to weave Type 2 on the pattern heddle—it's just a matter of personal preference.

Pointed shuttle to carry the weft, for beating, and for making pick-ups in some weaves. When I'm making pick-ups with my fingers (Type 2 on the band heddle) I use a double-pointed netting shuttle. When I'm making pick-ups with the shuttle (Type 1 on the band heddle and Type 2 on the pattern heddle) I use a single-pointed netting shuttle with a longer point. Both shuttles are long enough to grasp with both hands for beating yet narrow and lightweight and easy to keep in my hands at all times.

Band clamp to attach the warp to the weaving belt. You can do without a band clamp and even without a weaving belt, by simply wrapping the band-in-progress around a flat stick, securing it with a safety pin, and tucking each end of the stick under a regular belt around your waist. But the band clamp makes it easier to advance the warp quickly as you weave and to apply tension more evenly across the width of the band. A separate **tie-on bar** is handy for getting the weaving started. I use a ⅜" dowel about 15" long for this, removing it as soon as I've woven enough of the band to insert into the band clamp.

Weaving belt to go around the weaver's waist and attach to the band clamp. You can improvise a weaving belt in many ways. I make my weaving belts with metal rings for durability, and ties so the belt stays in place when I hook and unhook the warp. A belt that drops off when you unhook the work is frustrating.

Warping pegs and clamps to hold them in place to measure and wind the warp with a cross. You can improvise with straight-backed chairs supported against the edge of the table or straight-legged chairs turned upside down at each end of the table.

Fig. 91: Tools and supplies. Clockwise from lower left: warping peg and clamp, weaving belt, scissors, band heddle, pattern heddle, cone holder, black clamp for holding heddle for threading, second warping peg and clamp, string for choke ties, shoelace for end of warp, and band clamp. At center, tape measure, tapestry needle and dental floss threaders, shuttles, and lease sticks.

Fig. 92: An inexpensive milk crate set on end works with the cone holder as a yarn feeder. The yarn unwinds smoothly when it travels straight up before being pulled to the side.

Cone holder for holding cones or tubes upright as you warp. Jars or baskets will keep round balls from rolling around. Place the cone holder or jars inside a **milk crate** so the yarn feeds straight up before it gets pulled to the side to help it unwind smoothly, as shown in Fig. 92.

Lease sticks for holding the cross in the warp while you thread the heddle. Mine are cut from an extra Glimåkra warp stick from my floor loom. They are 7" long, ¾" wide and a little more than ⅛" thick, with small holes drilled in each end so they can be connected with string. Exact dimensions are not important, but the sticks should be lightweight and smoothly-sanded.

Heavy cotton cooking twine or similar for tying choke ties and fastening the lease sticks together. Seal the ends with white glue so they won't ravel. A **shoelace** is handy for tying the end of the warp to a fixed point for weaving.

Clamp to hold the heddle flat at the edge of a table for threading, either a bar clamp with soft pads or a C-clamp with added felt pads. The clamp can also provide a means to attach the warp to a fixed shelf or heavy piece of furniture for weaving, if a doorknob or similar fixed point is not available.

You'll also need **dental floss threaders** from the drugstore for threading the holes and slots in the heddle, a small **tapestry needle**, **scissors**, **ruler**, **tape measure**, and **masking tape**.

Yarn and Color

For the bands in this book I used the following yarns:

Perle (or Pearl) Cotton size 5/2 (about 2100 yards per pound). Used for warp and weft in the all-cotton plain and pick-up bands that I often call ribbons. This yarn is easy to work with, available from most weaving suppliers, and makes a nice ribbon or band.

Rauma Prydvevgarn and **Hifa Frid Vevgarn** (both about 1500 yards per pound), lustrous and sturdy two-ply Norwegian weaving yarns spun from all or part Norwegian Spelsau wool. Used for pattern warp in both Type 1 and Type 2 pick-up.

Bockens Cotton size 8/2 (about 3200 yards per pound), an unmercerized Swedish yarn spun from long-staple cotton. Used for background warp and weft with wool pattern warp in Type 2 pick-up.

Maysville Cotton size 8/4 (about 1600 yards per pound), an unmercerized cotton yarn about the same weight as Rauma Prydvevgarn and Hifa Frid Vevgarn. Used with those wools for some bands in Type 1 as a substitute for the thick cotton used in many old Norwegian bands.

Choosing other yarns

In choosing a yarn suitable for bandweaving, look for one that is strong and smooth, without nubs and slubs. Warp-faced weaving is more demanding of yarn than many other kinds of weaving because of increased friction between closely-set warp ends and because the weft is pulled firmly to keep the edges neat. Most singles and lightly-twisted knitting yarns aren't suitable, and loosely-spun 8/2 cottons aren't strong enough either. Fuzzy, woolen-spun yarns are more difficult to work with than smooth, worsted-spun yarns.

Thickness of background and pattern warp

For Type 1, both pattern colors should be the same thickness. For Type 2, the pattern yarn should be at least twice as thick as the background yarn. For Type 2 bands in perle cotton, a double strand is used for the pattern color. For Type 2 bands in cotton and wool, the wool is about twice as thick as the cotton and is used single strand.

Weft

In Type 1, the weft is traditionally the same yarn and color as the border warp. In Type 2, the weft is traditionally the same yarn and color as the background warp.

Fiber choices and combinations

Most traditional Norwegian bands were woven in a combination of wool and linen or wool and cotton. Some were woven in all wool. Today, we might choose to use all cotton or all linen, depending on the end use and the appearance we want.

Fig. 93: Choosing yarn. Perle cotton at left, Hifa Frid Vevgarn and Maysville Cotton at center, and Rauma Prydvevgarn and Bockens Cotton at right.

Fig. 94: The rust and white plain-weave band in perle cotton is perfect for a first project. The black and white band shows other designs that are possible in plain weave by varying the order of colors in the warp.

I've used perle cotton for the narrow bands. Since mercerized cotton was not available until the late 1800s, it was not used in the old farm society, but it was adopted by some traditional weavers after that. Aagot Noss writes that Ingebjørg Berdal, born in 1890, learned to weave from her mother, wore traditional folk dress, and wove her own hairbands in pick-up using *perlegarn* (perle cotton yarn).[4] And perle cotton is sometimes used for the background color in bands woven for the Vest-Telemark bunad.

Colors

Type 2 traditionally used red for pattern and natural cotton or linen for background, with borders and accents in other colors like black, blue, green, brown, gold, and yellow. In my narrow bands I've used blue and green in addition to rust and red for pattern colors, though I've followed the traditional rule of light background and dark pattern for Type 2. In Type 1 sometimes both colors were darker, such as black with red. In choosing the colors and combinations that appeal to you, keep in mind that the patterns will stand out best if there is strong value contrast between the background and pattern colors for Type 2 and between the two pattern colors for Type 1.

About the Sample Bands

In the sample bands for this book I have not tried to duplicate historical Norwegian bands. I've used pattern charts created from bands in museum collections, but in weaving the bands in perle cotton I haven't used those pattern charts with the same colors and border designs as in the originals. In the wool and cotton bands, my choices for colors and border designs are in keeping with tradition, though I've made no attempt to copy original bands there either.

Planning Warp Lengths

When planning warp lengths, you'll need to consider not only the desired finished length of your piece, but also shrinkage, take-up, and loom waste.

Shrinkage: You'll need to weave the band longer than the desired length to allow for shrinkage. The amount of shrinkage varies depending on yarn, technique, and washing method. I estimate the woven length will shrink 5–8% after hand washing in warm water, and add 10% of the desired length to the warp length so I can allow for this.

Take-up: The warp travels in a serpentine path over and under the weft, and also relaxes when it's no longer held under tension, so a woven band is always shorter than the starting warp length. The amount of take-up will vary depending on how you beat and what kind of yarn you use for warp and weft. For pick-up bands I add about 20% of the desired finished length.

Loom waste: I allow 9" at the beginning of a warp, for trimming the warp before threading, tying on, and weaving an inch or two to properly space and tension the warp. I allow 18" for unwoven warp at the end, more if the band is wider than 1". You can get by with less but it's harder to maintain good selvedges and an even warp density when you have to weave too close to the heddle where the warp ends are spread out. If the band will be fringed, loom waste can be used for that.

Total: These factors vary from weaver to weaver and project to project, so keep records to help in planning future bands. And when in doubt make the warp longer than you think you'll need. A quick rule of thumb is to add 30% plus 27" to the desired length of the finished woven piece.

How to Read a Warp Draft

The warp drafts referred to throughout this **Part** are shown in Fig. 151. A warp draft shows the number of warp ends and the order of colors in the warp, represented by symbols. The two horizontal rows on the draft represent the two alternating threading positions necessary for plain weave, which on the band heddle are holes and slots. It doesn't matter which row you choose to represent holes and which to represent slots. That will depend on how you center the warp in the band heddle and whether you begin with a hole or a slot, as described in the next section. This format simply reminds you to alternate holes and slots as you thread.

You refer to the warp draft to wind the warp in the correct color order. For Warp Draft 1 in Fig. 151, you would use two colors, winding 4 ends of the first color, 2 ends of the second color, 1 end of the first, and so forth across, for a total of 35 ends. The winding method described below preserves the color order, so you can simply thread the colors in the band heddle in the same order, alternating holes and slots.

Some warp drafts for pick-up specify a doubled strand for the pattern color. In that case, you wind two strands of that color but thread them both through the same hole or slot so they act as one double-thick strand. If the pattern yarn you are using is already twice as thick as the background yarn, you can simply wind one strand instead of two.

A First Project

A suggested first project is a plain-weave band like the one shown in Fig. 94 in rust and natural white, woven with Warp Draft 1 in Fig. 151. I used 5/2 perle cotton for a width of about ¾". A warp three yards long gives plenty of allowance for shrinkage, take-up, loom waste, and practice, as well as a finished band long enough to knot in a loop to hold scissors around your neck, which is one idea for using the finished band.

If you want to use a different order of colors in the warp, keep in mind that in plain weave the order of colors determines the design you see in the band. The basic design elements are stripes (two or more adjacent ends in the same color), bars (alternating ends in two colors), and dashed lines or flecks (a single end of one color). These elements can be combined to make ladders, serrated stripes, and flecked patterns, as shown in the black and white band in Fig. 94. Using more than two colors opens up more possibilities for design.

Warping the Heddle

Warping the heddle is a simple, two-step process: First you'll wind the warp around pegs so that all the ends are the correct length and in the right color order. Then you'll thread the ends through the holes and slots in the heddle.

Setting up to wind the warp

Clamp each warping peg to a table. The distance between them is the desired warp length. Peg 1 on the left will hold the end of the warp that will be threaded through the heddle. Peg 2 on the right will hold the end of the warp that will be tied to a fixed point during weaving. Place the yarn on the floor between the pegs. It should be packaged so it unwinds freely. Put cones, tubes, or spools on a cone holder to keep them from tipping over and getting tangled. Put round balls in jars or baskets. Feed each end of yarn up through a hole in the milk crate directly above the cone or ball. The crate, although optional, acts as a yarn feeder for smoother unwinding and makes the process more pleasant. With more than two colors I use two cone holders and two milk crates. Be sure to set the milk crate on the side of the warp towards you. If you put it under the warp or on the side away from you things will get tangled. Have your warp draft and a pencil handy to check off the number of warp ends and the order of colors as you go. Place scissors on a ribbon around your neck for easy color changes at either peg.

Fig. 95: Winding the warp around two warping pegs in a figure-eight forms a cross between the pegs. The distance between the pegs determines the length of the warp.

Winding the warp

For an odd number of warp ends, begin at Peg 2. For an even number, begin at Peg 1. This way the cut end of the last warp end will be at Peg 1 where the ends will be cut anyway prior to threading. Tie a secure loop with an overhand knot in the first color and slip the loop over the starting peg. Wind the yarn around the pegs in a figure-eight (see Fig. 95), always winding around the far side of the peg first so that a cross forms between the pegs. This is very important to preserve the order of the warp until threading is complete.

One trip from Peg 1 to Peg 2 or vice versa equals one warp end. Follow the color order for your particular warp. Change colors at either peg as required by the warp color order, by cutting the old color and tying the new one to it, as close to the peg as possible, with a secure knot like an overhand knot. As you wind, do not pull tightly. Simply lay the yarn around the pegs, taking up the slack and keeping a relaxed, even tension. If you need to set down the thread in your hand to pick up another color, you can wrap it around the peg several times to temporarily secure it, or you can cut it a few inches past the peg and hold it to the peg with a bit of masking tape. This keeps the warp neat and under control at all times. When you have wound the last warp end you should be back at Peg 1. Temporarily fasten the yarn to the peg with a few wraps or with tape.

Securing the warp

To preserve the cross, slip the lease sticks into the open spaces held by the pegs. Slide the lease sticks toward the center of the warp until they meet. Tie the sticks together with string, then slide both lease sticks until they are about 18" away from Peg 1 to put them into position for threading. Tie a choke tie around the warp bundle a couple of inches from Peg 1, by wrapping tightly with heavy string and ending with a firm bow knot, to keep the end loop of the warp neat and secure until you cut it prior to threading. Tie another choke tie about a yard from Peg 1, to make a secure point on which to place a heavy box or other weight during threading. Put a shoelace through the end loop at Peg 2 and tie it with a firm square knot. Later you'll use the shoelace to tie the warp to a fixed point for weaving. Also tie a choke tie a couple of inches away from the shoelace around the whole warp bundle to further secure this end (this is the only choke tie that stays until you've finished weaving). If your warp is longer then 3 yards, tie more choke ties about a yard apart to keep the warp neat and secure. Check to make sure the cross is securely preserved on the lease sticks (see Fig. 96 and Fig. 97) before removing the warp from the pegs. Trim off the knots at Peg 1 so all the ends are cut and there are no loops at that end.

Setting up to thread the heddle

Clamp the heddle to the edge of a table so that it is held securely and you can access the holes and slots for threading. If the heddle has a right side, place it face down with the top edge facing you. Lay the warp bundle behind the heddle with the cross end closest to you and the lease sticks about a foot away.

Place a weight on the choke tie that is a yard away from the end. Remove the choke tie near the cut end.

Centering the warp

It is important to center the warp so the heddle will be balanced. For example, if your band heddle has 51 total spaces (holes and slots) and you have 35 working ends in your warp, you will have eight empty spaces on each side. So you would skip four holes and four slots, and begin threading in the fifth hole from the right. If your band heddle has 41 spaces and you have 35 working ends in your warp, you will have three empty spaces on each side and begin threading in the second slot from the right. Whether you start the warp in a hole or a slot doesn't matter as long as the warp is centered. On the pattern heddle you might prefer to begin threading in the middle, placing the center pattern end in the center pattern slot and working out from there on both sides to automatically center the warp.

Threading the heddle

If you thread from right to left, hold the warp under tension with your left hand while you pick off the rightmost warp end from the cross, as shown in Fig. 98. Thread that end through the loop of the floss threader, then take the floss threader down through the hole or slot that you have determined as your

Fig. 96: Sample warp wound on pegs and ready to take off for threading, with lease sticks and choke ties in position. An actual warp would be much longer, perhaps wound between two tables, with additional choke ties every yard or so between the lease sticks at left and the shoelace at the right end.

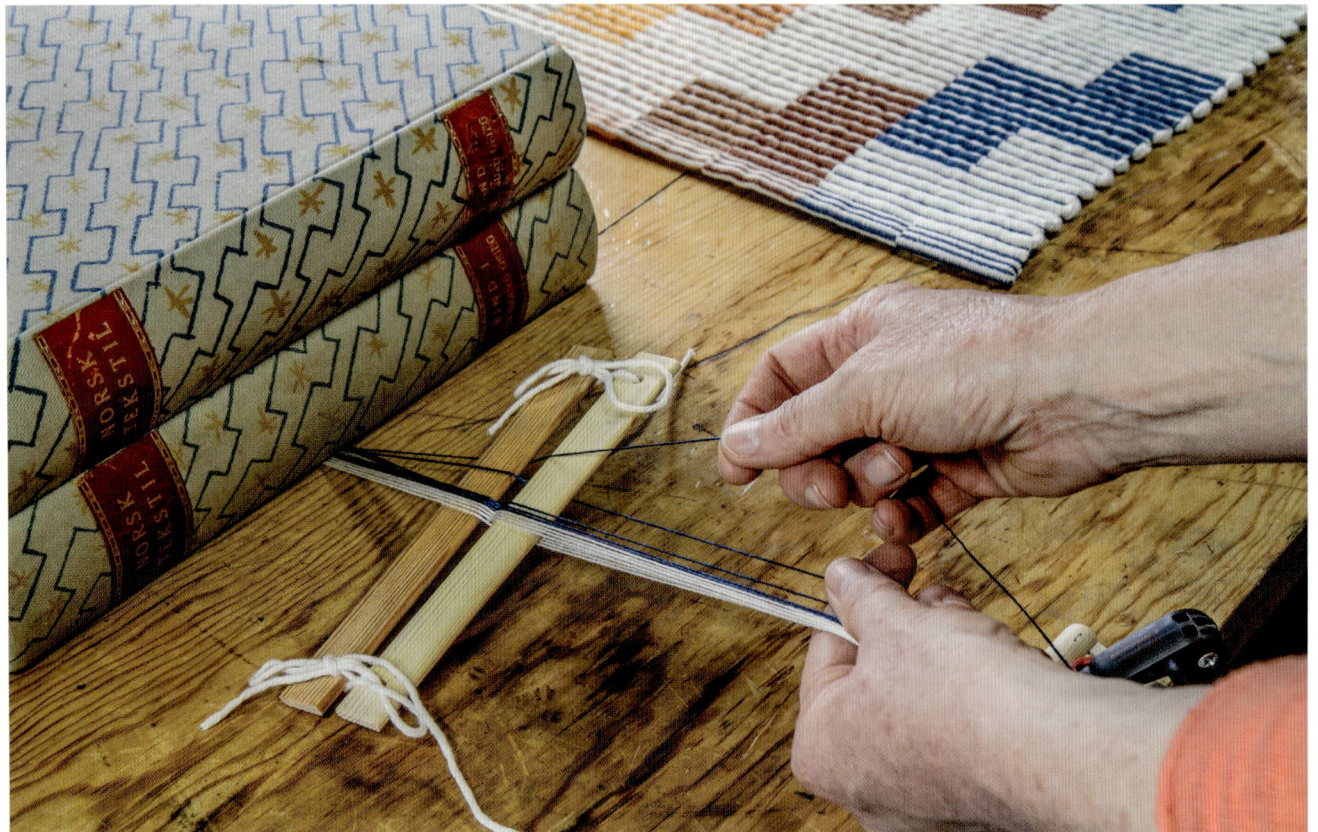

starting point, as shown in Fig. 99. Continue taking the warp ends in order from the cross at the lease sticks and threading them in order in the heddle, always alternating holes and slots. When you are finished, temporarily secure the warp by tying all the ends in a large slip knot so they won't pull out of the heddle accidentally.

Threading for pick-up

Sometimes pick-up pattern ends are doubled and two ends of the same color will be threaded through the same hole or slot. When threading a pattern heddle for pick-up, thread the border ends and the background ends through regular holes and slots and the pattern ends through the pattern slots.

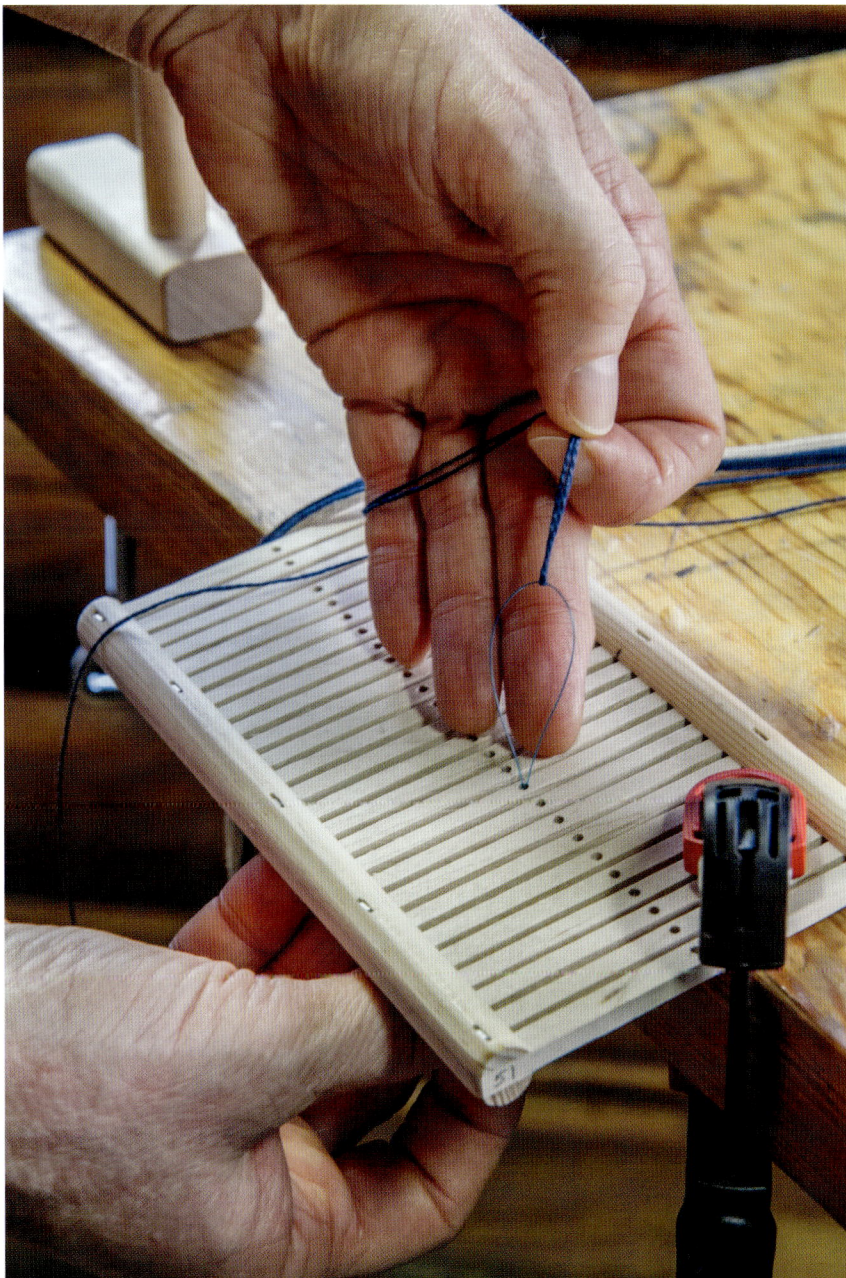

(Opposite Page) Fig 97: Lease sticks in position. A cross forms between the warping pegs when you wind around them in a figure-eight. The cross is held securely by the lease sticks to preserve the order of the warp until the heddle is threaded.

(Opposite page) Fig. 98: Threading the warp ends in order. Heavy books anchor the warp to make it easier to pick off the ends one by one from the cross and thread them through the heddle.

Fig. 99: Threading the heddle. Clamping the heddle to the table so it lies horizontally makes it easy to see what you're doing. I've put the blue end through the loop of the dental floss threader, which also happens to be blue, and I'm taking it down through a hole in the heddle.

Weaving Basics

Setting up to weave

Put on your weaving belt. I place mine just below the waist. Wind a shuttle with weft yarn. Tie the far end of the warp to a fixed point like a door knob or a bar clamp attached to something that won't move. Place your chair near the other end of the warp. If your warp is three yards or less, take out all choke ties except for the one at the far end. If your warp is longer than three yards, you can leave the choke ties on the additional length for now. If you don't have room to stretch out the entire warp length, make a lark's head knot in the warp bundle behind a choke tie and attach that to the fixed point.

Comb the warp bundle with the heddle to neaten it and make sure it isn't twisted. Take out the temporary slip knot you tied after threading the heddle and slide the heddle an arm's length away. Carefully stroke and comb the warp with your fingers so all the ends are as evenly tensioned as possible.

Tying on

To attach the warp to the weaving belt to get started, I put a tie-on bar (a 15" dowel) through the rings of my weaving belt and tie the warp directly to that. To do this, divide the warp ends into two sections, bring them over

Fig. 100: Tying the warp to a tie-on bar placed through the rings of the weaving belt. The far end of the warp is already tied to a fixed object with a shoelace. This is the first half of a square knot.

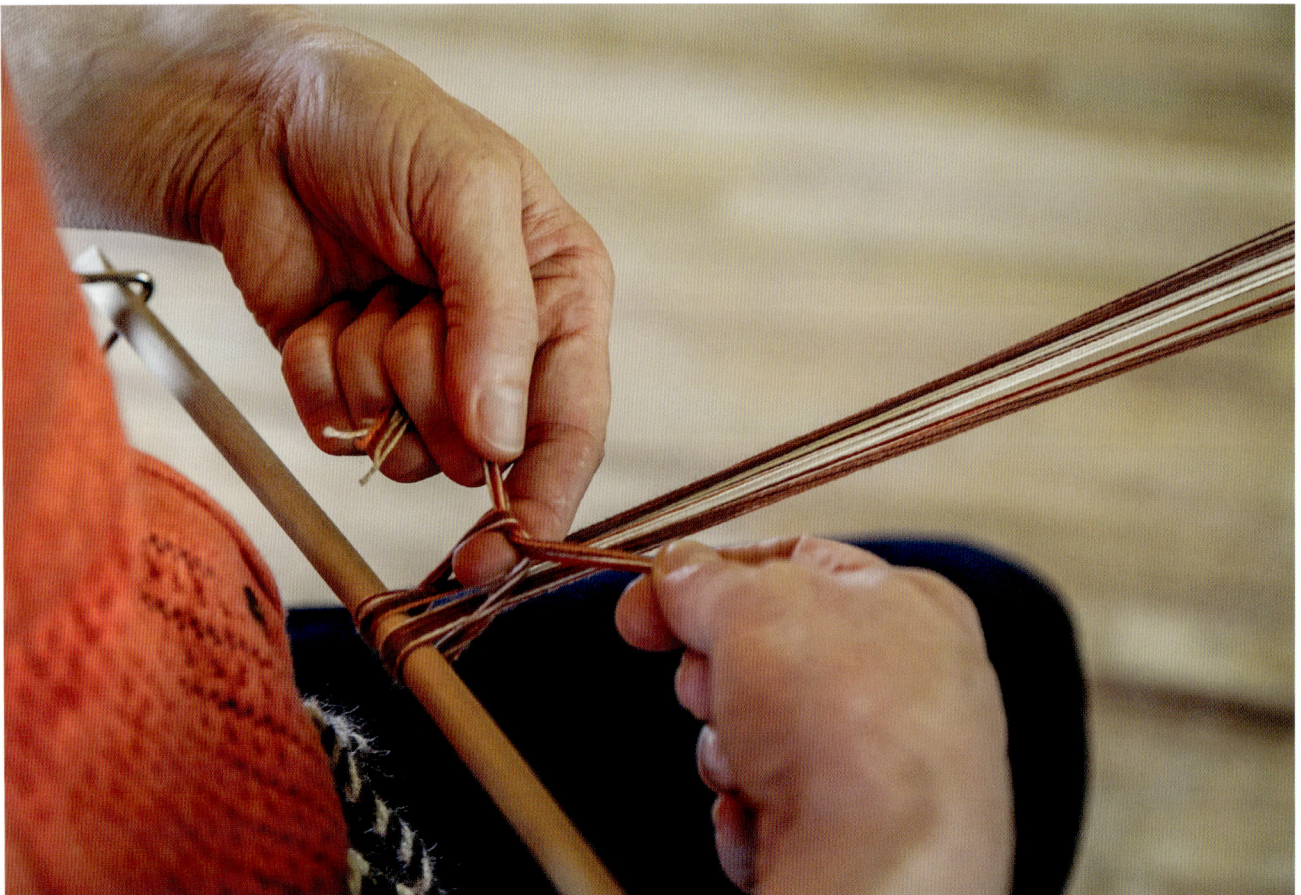

the bar towards you, then around the bar and under it away from you. Bring one section up on each side of the warp and tie a square knot with the two sections on top of the warp and snug against the bar. See Fig. 100. As you tie on, position your chair so you can put tension on the warp with your body.

Putting in spacers

I use three narrow strips of cardstock or lightweight cardboard as spacers to weave three rows in the beginning, as shown in Fig. 101. This helps spread the warp to an appropriate width. Make a shed, place a strip, change sheds, beat lightly with the edge of your hand, place a second strip, and so forth. Pull the spacers out after you've woven a few rows with regular weft.

Weaving the first few rows with regular weft

Change sheds and take the shuttle through, leaving a tail of weft a few inches long at the selvedge. Change sheds, beat the previous row into place with the edge of the shuttle, and take the shuttle through, pulling the weft snugly around the ends at the selvedge. Change sheds and continue in this way. After three rows the weft will have encircled the edge warp ends on both sides and it will be easier to keep the weaving neat. If these rows aren't neat you can pull them out after the band is off the heddle.

Fig. 101: Putting in spacers. I've placed strips of folded cardstock in the sheds to space the warp and make it easier to begin weaving with weft yarn.

Fig. 102: Making a down-shed for plain weave. I'm pushing down the heddle with my left hand while I insert the shuttle into the shed near the heddle where the shed is the largest. As soon as the shuttle is in the shed I can take my hand off the heddle and pull the shuttle through.

Being consistent in the direction you start the shuttle

I always weave the down-shed from right to left and the up-shed from left to right. You could do the opposite, but it's important to be consistent. That way you'll always know which shed you're on from the position of your shuttle. See Fig. 102.

Using the band clamp

When you've woven about four inches you can slip out the tie-on bar, insert the partially-woven band into the band clamp, and continue that way. Holding the clamp with the hooks pointing away from you, feed the band down between the two halves of the clamp and center it, leaving a few inches of woven band extending at the top. Press the two halves of the clamp firmly together as you roll the clamp up and around so the hooks are now pointing towards you and you can attach them to your belt. Ideally the fell line should be just in front of the band clamp.

Advancing the warp

Every couple of inches you'll need to advance the warp to bring the fell line closer to the clamp. This keeps a good distance between the fell line and the heddle, which is always held at arm's length. Lean forward slightly to relax the tension on the band clamp. As you do so, grab the band that is extending from underneath the clamp with both hands and pull away from yourself. Hold the clamp securely while you scoot your chair forward to compensate for the shortened warp.

Keeping the heddle an arm's length away

Always keep the heddle an arm's length away, as shown in Fig. 105. This puts a more even tension on the warp, making it easier to keep the width consistent and the selvedges neat as you weave.

Establishing a good width

As you weave, pull the weft so the warp ends lie smoothly side by side. They should cover the weft but not be bunched together. In warp-faced plain weave, the only place you should see the weft is where it turns to go into the next shed at the selvedge. Most new weavers do not pull the weft snugly enough in the beginning and then find that the band gets narrower as they weave. An ideal width is a range more than an absolute number. One weaver might pull a band in ⅛" more than another and both bands would look fine as long as the width was maintained.

Controlling the turn of the weft at the selvedge

Notice how the weft buckles a little after you beat, on the side where it exits the shed. This happens every time you beat and you correct it as you weave the following row. As you take the shuttle through the shed with one hand, pinch the weft between thumb and forefinger with the other hand near where it exits the previous row. Give the weft a little pull to neaten that edge. Then guide the weft into a sharp hairpin turn so it travels straight through the new

Fig. 103: Beating the weft into place. I'm holding the shuttle with both hands for even pressure and a balanced motion, pressing it against the fell line and rocking it slightly up and down to increase the beating action without applying much force.

Fig. 104: Controlling the turn of the weft. The weft is traveling straight through the shed. My right hand has pulled slightly to the right to neaten the point where the weft exits the previous row and I'm now guiding the weft into a sharp turn. As the loop becomes smaller I'll wiggle it a little to keep the warp ends neat at the selvedge, then let go and snug the turn up against the selvedge.

shed as shown in Fig. 104. There is no take-up in the weft and you need to place it snug against the fell line, not at an angle. As you pull the shuttle and the weft loop becomes smaller, wiggle the loop of weft so it neatly encircles the edge warp ends. Then let go of the turn and snug the weft up against the selvedge, lining up the new weft turn with the woven section below. When you stop to advance the warp you can use a ruler to check your width. If your edges are ragged or if you find yourself pulling on the weft again to correct the width after you've changed the shed, try pulling the weft more snugly as you weave. With practice, you'll be able to control the weft and keep the width consistent by feel.

Establishing a good weaving rhythm

The steps are the same on every row. For plain weave the steps are: change the shed, beat the previous row, neaten the weft where it comes out of the previous row and at the same time control the weft turn as you take the shuttle through the shed.

Beating firmly for a neat appearance

To beat, insert the shuttle in the shed, then pull it towards you with both hands, one on each side of the warp. As you press the near edge of the shuttle firmly against the fell line, rock the far edge of the shuttle up and down a little to pack the weft into place. See Fig. 103.

Anne Grete Stuksrud's tip

In Norway, our bandweaving teacher told us to ease our backs ever so slightly as we beat, to allow the warp the slack it needs to take up or encircle the weft in a serpentine fashion. This motion also makes it easier to beat because you're not using just your arms and shoulders. If you bring your waist forward slightly by putting a tiny bit more curve into your lower back as you pull the shuttle towards you, the beating becomes a coordinated motion between arms and lower torso, which is more relaxing and easier on the body. It's also important to sit up straight and not slouch over the work.

Maintaining the same tension

With practice you'll get a feel for maintaining a consistent tension with your body and this will help you achieve neat edges and an even beat. The warp doesn't need to be tight as a drum, and if it's too taut the edges will want to spread out and it will be harder to pull the warp in to an appropriate width. If it's too slack it will be hard to get a clean shed and the weaving won't be neat and even. I aim for a tension that is comfortable, neither too tight nor too loose.

Making a clean shed to prevent unwanted floats

Sometimes the warp ends catch on each other behind the heddle and prevent you from getting a clean shed. If you notice this happening, strum the warp with the tip of the shuttle or comb the warp back a short distance with the heddle.

Unhooking

To unhook the weaving to take a break, I put the shuttle into a shed, slide the heddle close to the shuttle, and clip the shuttle to the heddle with a clothespin so it won't fall out before setting everything down in a work basket. To pack a warp for travel, wrap the unwoven warp around the heddle to make a neat packet.

Joining in new weft

When you run out of weft, overlap the old and new weft yarns for a half inch or so in a shed, then bring the tails out through the warp in the lower level of the shed. Leave the tails a couple of inches long until the band is off the heddle. Then you can trim them flush with the back of the band.

Finishing the ends

When the band is finished, cut the warp, leaving an allowance for fringe if desired. At each end, thread the tail of weft into a small tapestry needle and weave it into the adjacent row, bringing it out the back about halfway across. Trim the tail flush with the back of the band. Fringe protects the weft and even a short fringe does the job since warp-faced bands don't ravel easily. If you don't want fringe, straight stitch across the ends of the band with a sewing machine before cutting. Then you can face the ends with wool felt, or fold them over twice to make hand-stitched hems, or tuck them into a seam on a sewing project.

Fig. 105: Always keep the heddle at arm's length as you weave, for more even tension.

Type 1 Pick-up on Band Heddle

In the threading for Type 1 pick-up, two pattern colors of the same thickness are threaded alternately—one in the holes and one in the slots—and either or both can be picked up to form patterns. In plain weave this threading yields alternating crosswise bars in the two pattern colors.

Winding a warp for Type 1—shortcut method

Since the threading calls for an alternating sequence of light/dark throughout the pattern area, you can hold both colors together as you wind, rather than cutting to change colors after each end. After you wind the border area in the normal way, cut that end and tie on both pattern colors. Hold the two pattern colors together between thumb and forefinger and separate them with your little finger as you wind. The two ends will lie together in the cross, but you will take them from the cross in the correct color order according to the warp draft—for example, always selecting the light end first and then the dark end from the pair at the cross.

Getting started

Warp your heddle according to Warp Draft 2 in Fig. 151. For the band shown in Fig. 106, I used 5/2 perle cotton in dark blue for the border, and rust and natural white for the two pattern colors. Wind a shuttle with weft in the border color. Put in the spacers, then weave a few rows in plain weave with the weft yarn to establish a good width. The band will narrow a little when the pick-up pattern begins, because the fabric structure is less dense where pattern ends are floating. My band is a little less than ½" wide. Be consistent in the direction you start the shuttle (down shed always right to left, for example).

Fig. 106: The Type 1 warp in progress was used to weave the cotton ties for the weaving belt and is also the one referred to in the row-by-row instructions for Type 1 pick-up. The zigzag-patterned band is the one referred to in the row-by-row instructions for Type 2 pick-up. The band to its left shows an alternate threading that gives a whipstitched look to the selvedges. The weaving belt is sewn from heavy-duty 2" cotton webbing, with triangle rings for attaching to the band clamp.

Fig. 107: Chart for band in Type 1 pick-up.

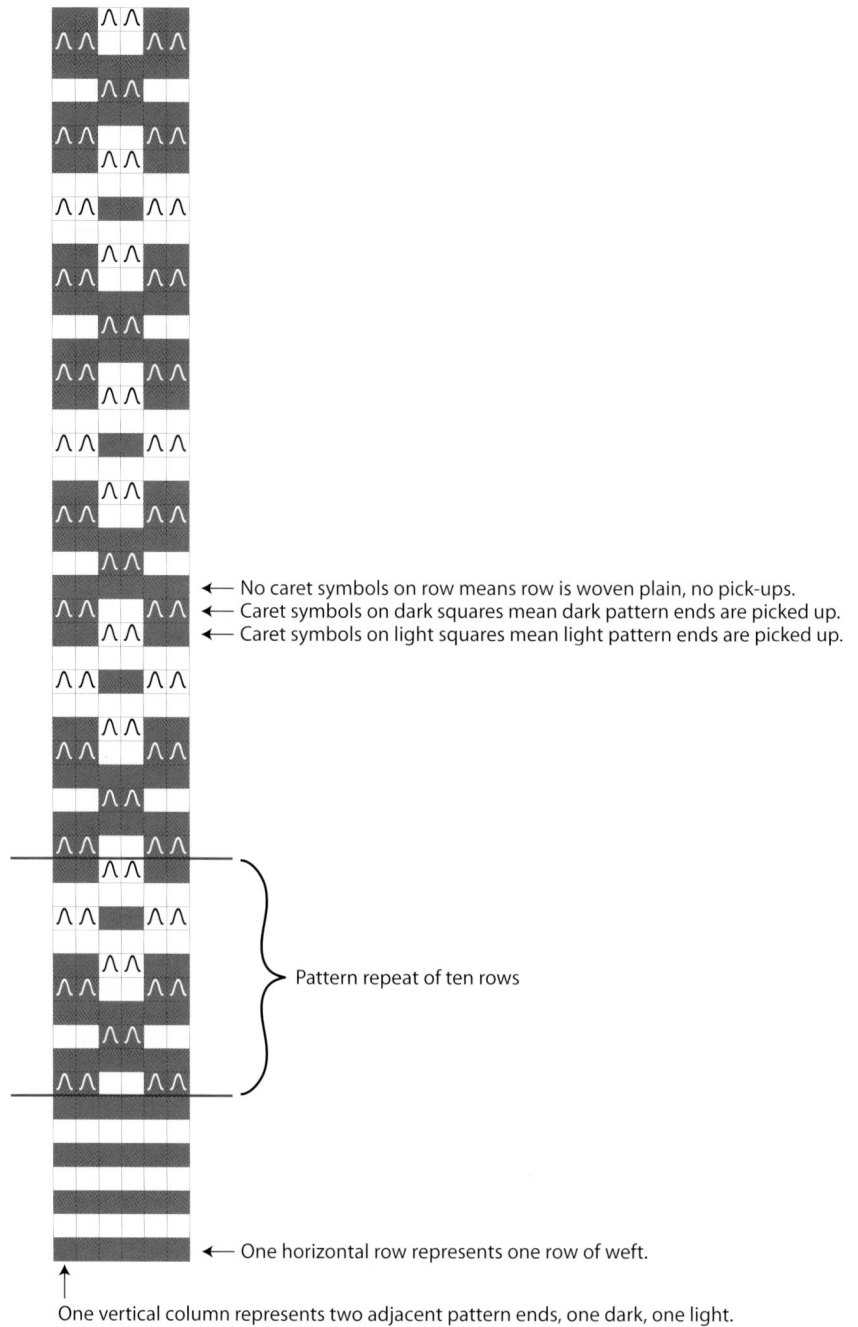

← No caret symbols on row means row is woven plain, no pick-ups.
← Caret symbols on dark squares mean dark pattern ends are picked up.
← Caret symbols on light squares mean light pattern ends are picked up.

Pattern repeat of ten rows

← One horizontal row represents one row of weft.

One vertical column represents two adjacent pattern ends, one dark, one light.

Reading the pattern chart

The chart used for the following row-by-row instructions is shown in Fig. 107. It is read from bottom to top, in the same direction the weaving proceeds. One horizontal row of squares represents one row of weft. At the bottom are the alternating dark and light bars of pattern color that occur when the warp is woven in plain weave. This shows how the first motif lies in relation to the first few rows of plain weave at the beginning of the band. Charts are drawn on a square grid, but patterns usually appear more elongated when woven.

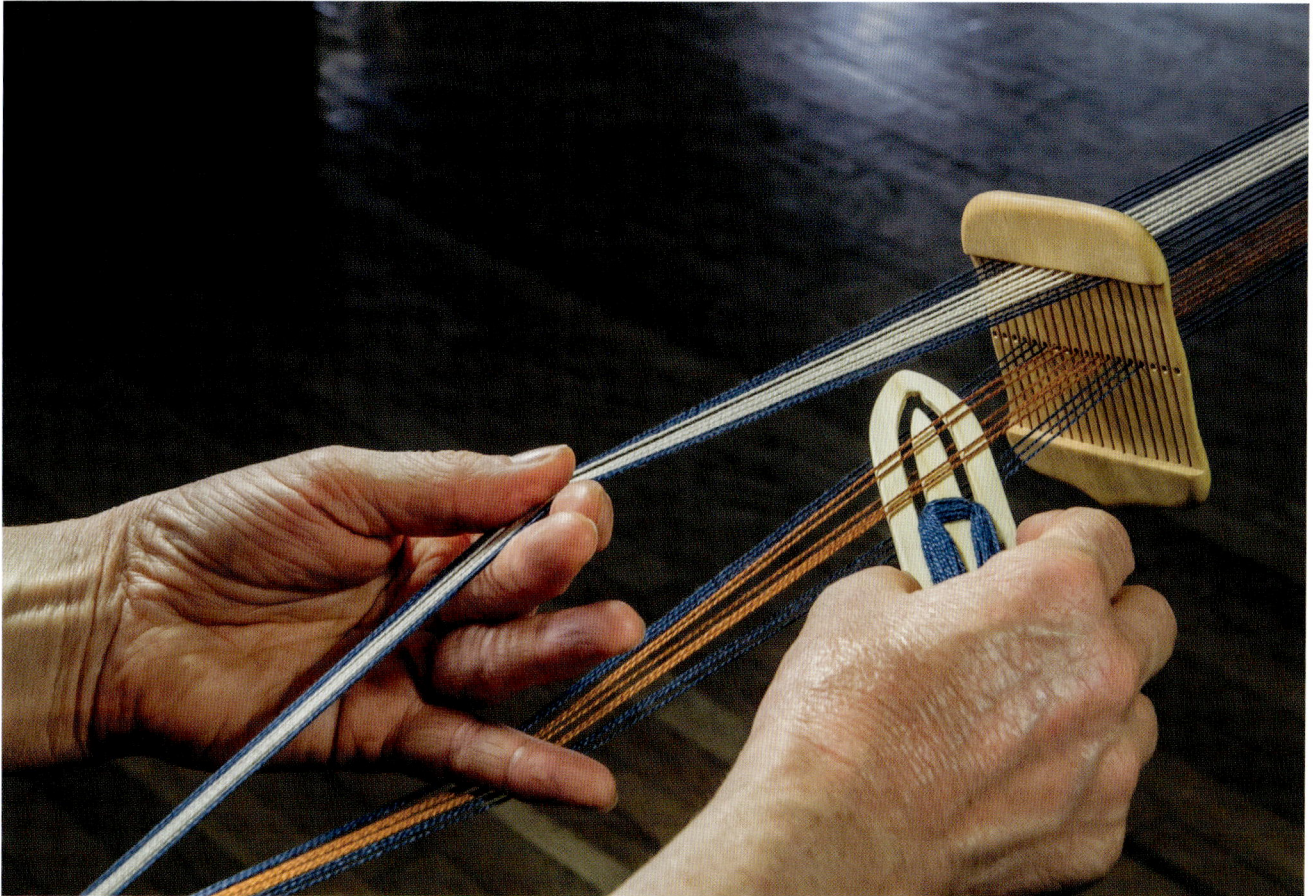

Type 1 pick-up is easy to do, but the pattern charts might seem confusing at first. This is because one vertical column on the graph paper represents two pattern ends—a light pattern end and the dark pattern end immediately adjacent to it. A dark square means the dark pattern end is on the surface on that row, and a light square means the light pattern end is on the surface on that row. Fortunately, the weaving itself is not confusing. All pick-ups are made when the pattern color in question is in the lower level of the shed, and since only one pattern color is in the lower level on any given row, you can't go wrong by selecting the wrong color. This will become clear as you follow the row-by-row instructions.

One repeat of the pattern is marked in red. A caret symbol shows that a pattern end is picked up on that row. If the caret symbol is in a dark square it means that the dark pattern end is picked up, and if the caret symbol is in a light square it means that the light pattern end is picked up. Rows with no caret symbols are woven plain, without pick-ups.

Beginning on the correct shed

On any given shed, one pattern color is up, in the upper level of the shed, and the other is down, in the lower level. You'll be ready to begin the first pick-up when you are ready to weave the shed that brings the dark pattern ends down.

Fig. 108: Making a pick-up with the shuttle. I'm holding the down-shed open with my left hand, tipping it slightly so I can see inside the shed, and with the point of the shuttle I've selected the two pairs I want to pick up from the lower level of the shed.

Row-by-row instructions

There are six dark pattern ends and six light pattern ends. We'll pick up each color in pairs, so it helps to think of these ends as three dark pairs and three light pairs.

Making the pick-ups: Beat the previous row but do not take the weft through. Instead, take the shuttle back out of the shed, slipping your other hand into the shed to hold it open. Tip that hand up on the shuttle side so you can see inside the shed near the heddle. Try not to set the shuttle down at any point, but keep it in your hand for greater efficiency. Take the point of the shuttle under the correct pattern pairs as noted in the following instructions. It's easiest to make the pick-ups near the heddle, where the ends are clearly separated from their neighbors and evenly spaced. See Fig. 108.

Row 1: The dark pattern ends are down. Pick up the two outside dark pairs by going under them with the point of the shuttle. In other words, pick up the first two dark pattern ends (one outside pair), then skip the next two dark pattern ends (the center pair), and pick up the last two dark pattern ends (the other outside pair). Then take the shuttle through the shed.

Row 2: Weave plain. No pick-up is necessary on this row.

Row 3: Pick up the center dark pair.

Row 4: Weave plain.

Row 5: Pick up the outside dark pairs as you did in Row 1.

Row 6: Pick up the center light pair.

Row 7: Weave plain.

Row 8: Pick up the outside light pairs.

Row 9: Weave plain.

Row 10: Pick up the center light pair.

Continue weaving this ten-row repeat. Notice how what you are doing relates to the chart, so that after a few repeats you'll understand the weave structure and be able to weave just by looking at the band, without referring to the chart.

This pattern is used for the borders in many bands from Telemark and is called the *geiteklauv* (goat's hoof) pattern.

Type 1 pattern options

On wider bands isolated motifs in one or both pattern colors can be woven, leaving the crosswise bars formed by the threading visible around the motifs. But usually the entire surface of the pattern area is covered with floats in both patterns colors. Bands 2 and 17 in **Part 2** are examples of this.

In an interesting threading variation for Type 1, the color sequence shifts from light/dark in one section to dark/light in the next, and so forth, and charts for this variation are given in the Pattern Supplement at the end of this **Part**. Although the patterns look complex they are easy to weave.

Reading a chart without symbols

When you see either a dark or a light float over three rows, you know that the end in that color is picked up to make the float on the middle row of the span. If none of the squares on a particular row are in the middle of a 3-row span in either color, then that row is woven plain.

Type 2 Pick-up on Band Heddle

In the threading for Type 2 pick-up, the thicker pattern ends are always separated by two finer background ends. Only the pattern ends are picked up, never the background ends. In plain weave this threading yields alternating flecks in the pattern color.

Getting started

Warp your heddle according to Warp Draft 3 in Fig. 151. For the zigzag-patterned band shown in Fig. 106, I used 5/2 perle cotton in natural white for

Fig. 109: A cotton ribbon tied around a gift of gloves and stockings. The man's sweater on the cover of the vintage knitting pattern is trimmed with a pick-up band. Knitting pattern ©Sandnes Garn AS, Norway.

Fig. 110: A wool and cotton band with seven pattern ends forms a hanging loop for a stick used to make *lefse* (a Norwegian treat made from thinly-rolled dough). This combination of Bockens Cotton 8/2 and Hifa Frid Vevgarn yields a narrower band than one in 5/2 perle cotton with the same number of warp ends.

background, rust for borders, and dark blue for pattern. Wind a shuttle with weft yarn in the background color. Put in the spacers, then weave a few rows in plain weave with the weft yarn to establish a good width. The band will narrow a little when the pick-up pattern begins, because the fabric structure is less dense where pattern ends are floating. My band is ⅝" wide. Be consistent in the direction you start the shuttle (down shed always right to left, for example).

You could also use Warp Draft 4 in Fig. 151 for this band, for the whipstitched edge variation on the second band shown in Fig. 106. I used 5/2 perle cotton for this band, in natural white and dark blue, for a width of a little more than ½". If you do use this alternate draft, take care not to confuse the colored border threads on each side with the outermost pattern ends.

Reading the pattern chart

The chart for the zigzag pattern used in the following row-by-row instructions is shown in Fig. 111. Charts are read from bottom to top, the same direction the weaving proceeds. One vertical column represents one pattern end. Background ends are not represented because they are never picked up or pushed down. One horizontal row of squares represents one row of weft. Charts are drawn on a square grid, but patterns usually appear more elongated when woven.

A dark square represents a pattern end that lies over the weft on that row and is visible on the front of the band. A light square represents a pattern end that lies under the weft on that row and is not visible on the front of the band. A caret symbol shows that the pattern end is picked up on that row. An X symbol shows that the pattern end is pushed down on that row.

At the bottom of the chart are the flecks of pattern color in a checkerboard arrangement that occur when the threading is woven in plain weave. This shows how the motif lies in relation to the first few rows of plain weave at the beginning of the band.

Beginning the pattern on the correct shed

Pick-ups are always made when the pattern ends in question are in the lower level of the shed. The odd-numbered pattern ends (1, 3, 5, and 7) are down on one shed and the even-numbered pattern ends (2, 4, and 6) are down on the next. Since the pattern for the sample band begins by picking up Pattern End 1, you will be ready to weave Row 1 when you change the shed and see that Pattern End 1 is down. If Pattern End 1 is up, weave another plain row.

Row-by-row instructions

Row 1: This first row of pick-up is the fourth row on the chart (the first three rows shown are plain weave). The twelve-row repeat marked is the one that is repeated later, after the pattern is underway, but first you'll need to segue from plain weave into the pattern as described here. The odd-numbered pattern ends are down. Beat the previous row with the shuttle but do not take the weft through the shed. Instead, take the shuttle back out of the shed, but keep the shuttle in your hand as you work for greater efficiency.

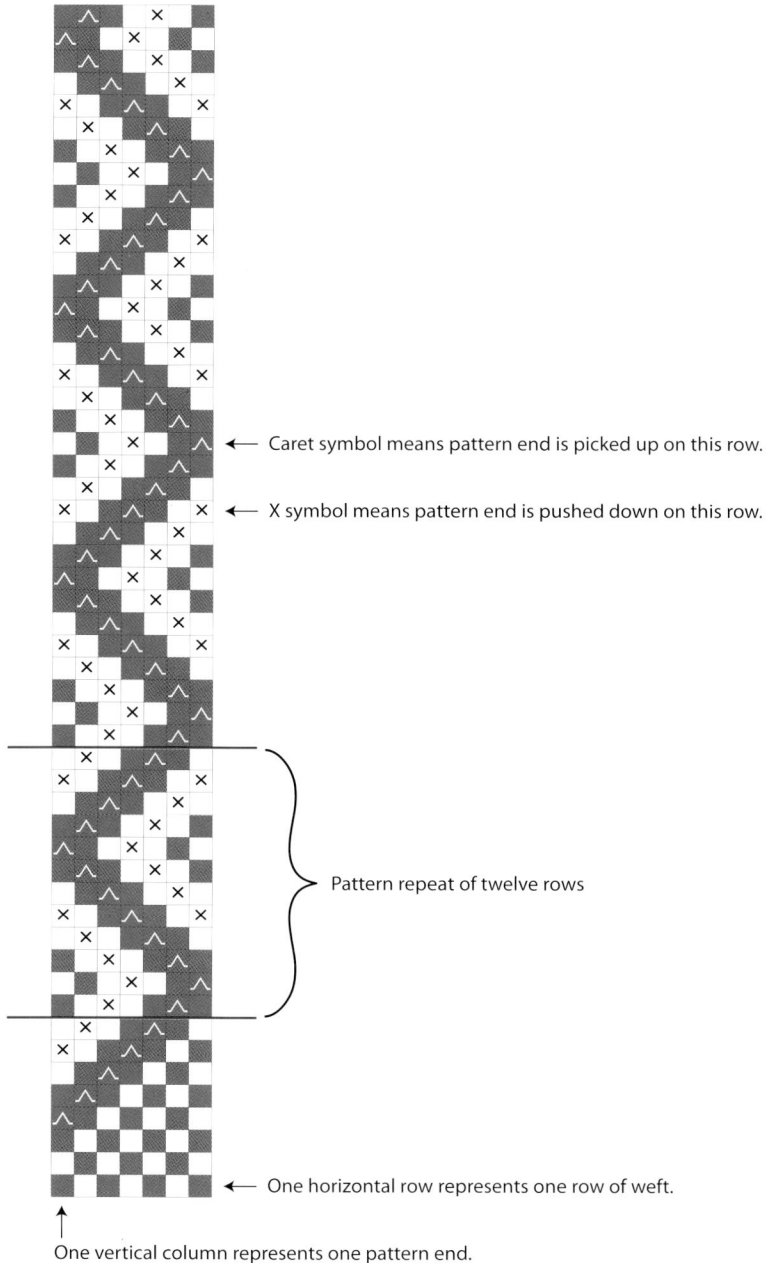

Fig. 111: Chart for band in Type 2 pick-up.

← Caret symbol means pattern end is picked up on this row.

← X symbol means pattern end is pushed down on this row.

Pattern repeat of twelve rows

← One horizontal row represents one row of weft.

One vertical column represents one pattern end.

Making a pick-up: Hold the shed open with both hands. Separate the upper level of the shed just above Pattern End 1, the first pattern end on the left. Reach down with an index finger, and pick up that pattern end so it is being held with the upper level of the shed. Take the hand that is holding the shuttle out of the shed, and hold the modified shed open with the other hand. Take the shuttle through the modified shed. Fig. 112 shows a pick-up being made, although it is not Pattern End 1.

Row 2: Make the next shed. Beat the previous row but do not take the weft through. Using the same hand motions as before, pick up Pattern End 2. Note that Pattern End 1 is in the upper level of the shed completing its float; leave it alone. Take the shuttle through the modified shed.

Fig. 112: Making a pick-up. I've made the shed, in this case the up-shed, and am keeping my hands in the shed to hold it open. I've separated the upper level of the shed on either side of the end in the lower level that I want to pick up, and I've reached down with an index finger to scoop up that end. Next, I'll bring it up so it lies in the upper level of the shed.

Follow the same sequence on every row: change sheds, beat the previous row but do not take the weft through, make any pick-ups or push-downs required by the pattern, hold the modified shed open with one hand and take the weft through with the other. Don't forget to pull on the weft to neaten the previous row as you take the weft through, the same as for plain weave.

Row 3: Pick up Pattern End 3. Note that Pattern End 2 is in the upper level of the shed completing its float; leave it alone. Also note that Pattern End 1 is in the lower level of the shed having completed its float; leave it alone.

Row 4: Pick up Pattern End 4. Also push down Pattern End 1, which is in the upper level of the shed.

Making a push-down: Separate the upper level of the shed on either side of Pattern End 1, reach out with your index finger and push down that pattern end so it is being held with the lower level of the shed. Fig. 113 shows a push-down being made, although it is not Pattern End 1. The modified shed you are holding open now has one pick-up and one push-down.

Row 5: Pick up Pattern End 5 and push down Pattern End 2.

Row 6: Pick up Pattern End 6 and push down Pattern End 3.

Row 7: Pick up Pattern End 7 and push down Pattern End 4.

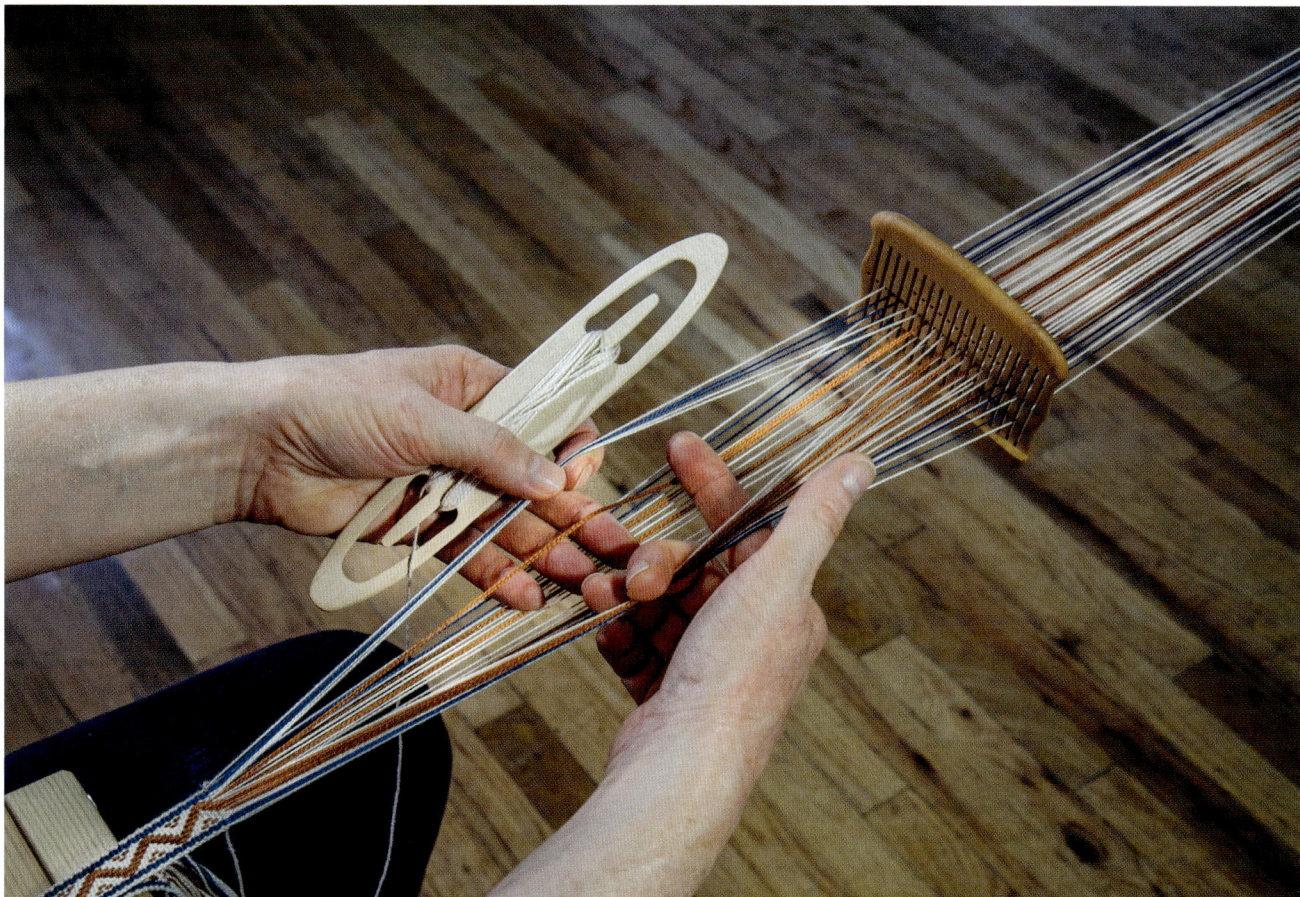

Row 8: Pattern End 6 is in the lower level of the shed, having completed its 3-row float. On this row you'll pick it up again in order to create a 5-row float and pivot the diagonal of the zigzag in the other direction. Pick up Pattern End 6 and push down Pattern End 3.

Row 9: Pick up Pattern End 5 and push down Pattern End 2.

Continue in this way to create a continuous zigzag. By watching what is happening as you follow the row-by-row instructions, and by comparing what you're doing to the chart, you'll quickly understand how patterns are created. Remember, never pick up or push down background ends. Pattern ends are the only ones you manipulate in making the modified shed. Also take care to always handle a doubled pattern end as one end, picking up or pushing down both strands together.

If you want to try other patterns on the sample warp, there are several charts for 7 pattern ends in the Pattern Supplement at the end of this **Part**, some of which show how to transition nicely between motifs.

Looking at the back

In Type 2 pick-up, the back is a reverse image of the front. Where motifs are formed by pick-ups on the front you see solid areas of background color on the back, and where solid areas of background color are formed by push-downs on the front, you see motifs formed by floats on the back. Either side can be used as the right side.

Fig. 113: Making a push-down. I've made the shed, in this case the up-shed, and am keeping my hands in the shed to hold it open. I've separated the upper level of the shed on either side of the end in the upper level that I want to push down, and I've put an index finger over that end. Next, I'll push it down so it lies in the lower level of the shed.

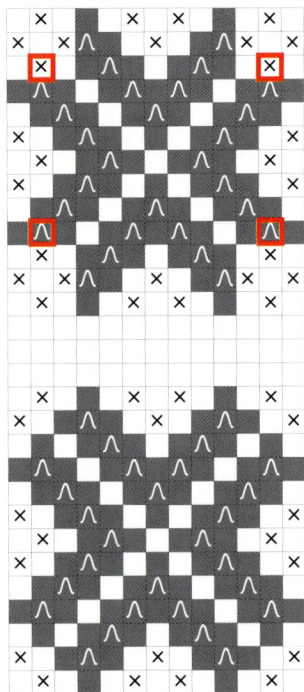

Fig. 114: Two forms of the eight-petaled rose. The one on top has horizontal lines, and the areas marked in red require close attention when woven on the band heddle.

Seeing the big picture

The motifs and background areas both develop naturally along stepped diagonal paths. Resist the temptation to place a ruler across the chart to isolate one row at a time, since to weave efficiently you need to keep your perspective and see the pattern as a whole.

Remember, you only have to pick up a pattern end once to create a 3-row float. On the first and third rows the pattern end is present on the front anyway because of the plain-weave interlacement, and you pick it up on the second row. Weavers who are new to pick-up sometimes think they have to push down floats, but floats will go down by themselves. The purpose of push-downs is only to "erase" plain-weave flecks before they have a chance to form. And you only have to "erase" a fleck once to create a 3-row area of background color. On the first and third rows, the pattern end is absent from the front anyway because of the plain-weave interlacement, and you push it down on the second row.

Pay special attention to which pattern ends are picked up twice to form 5-row floats and pivot diagonal lines in the motif. This will help you keep your place.

If you get confused when you're starting a complicated pattern you can isolate one row on the chart to double check. Once you've made all the pick-ups and push-downs on a certain row, the upper level of the shed should match that row on the chart. But it wouldn't be much fun to weave every row like this. That's why it helps to practice with simple patterns before trying more complex ones.

Reading a chart without symbols

When you see a float over three rows, you know a pick-up is made on the middle row of that span. And when you see a background area over three rows, you know a push-down is made on the middle row of that span.

Horizontal lines in motifs

In Type 2 pick-up, patterns develop naturally along stepped diagonal lines, but they can be modified to include horizontal lines. If a pattern has horizontal lines I prefer to weave it on the pattern heddle, because there I'm already thinking in terms of building the pattern in horizontal rows and all the pattern ends present themselves for selection on every row. It's not hard to weave horizontal lines on the band heddle, but you do have to pay close attention when weaving these areas, because they require you to do something that you never do when weaving regular diagonal patterns: you must pick up pattern ends that you just pushed down on the row before and you must push down pattern ends that you just picked up on the row before. Fig. 114 shows an eight-petaled rose, first with only stepped diagonal lines, then modified to include several horizontal lines, and the places that require close attention are marked.

Threading variation for Type 2 pick-up

A threading variation common in Setesdal and Vest-Agder yields diagonal pattern lines that are not as steep as with the normal Type 2 threading. Essentially, two pattern ends are paired with one background end between them, and the two are always picked up or pushed down together so they function as one unit. These units are separated by two background ends, as patterns ends are in the normal Type 2 threading, so the same kinds of patterns are possible but with a wider and less elongated appearance. Warp Draft 5 in Fig. 151 shows a threading with five units and Fig. 115 shows a zigzag motif that could be woven on this threading.

Type 2 Pick-up on Pattern Heddle

Floating pattern ends

The structure produced is the same whether you weave Type 2 pick-up on a band heddle or a pattern heddle, but the process is different. On the band heddle the pattern ends are threaded in plain weave along with the background ends, so a plain-weave structure is created automatically when you weave the two sheds. On the pattern heddle the pattern ends are not threaded in plain weave and they do not move up and down with the background ends when the sheds are made. Instead, they float in the middle of every shed and you decide which ones to select with a pointed shuttle before you weave the row.

In other words, you won't pick up and push down pattern ends as described for the band heddle. You'll get the same weave structure by selecting the pattern ends you want to show on the front on a given row and not selecting the pattern ends ones you don't want to show. This means that you must make a selection on every row, even for plain weave. This will become clear in the row-by-row instructions below.

Starting with the correct shed

On the first row, whether you begin with plain weave or pattern, you need to start with the correct shed, the one that will coordinate with the ends you're selecting. If you don't start with the correct shed, you'll notice that the pattern ends you selected aren't visible because they are hidden by the adjacent background ends. If you start with the wrong shed you can take out the row and start over with the other shed. But if you want to determine the correct shed before you begin, it's easy to do and this is explained below, after the row-by-row instructions.

Getting started

Warp your heddle according to Warp Draft 6 in Fig. 151. For the bands shown in Fig. 116, I used 5/2 perle cotton in natural white for background and red for pattern. The doubled pattern ends must be threaded through the pattern slots and the background ends in the regular holes and slots. Wind a shuttle with weft yarn in background color. Put in the spacers, then weave

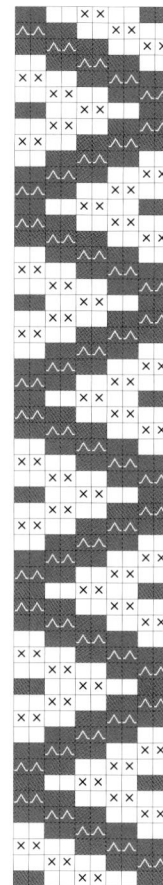

Fig. 115: Chart for zigzag pattern for Type 2 threading variation used in Setesdal.

Fig. 116: Type 2 bands. The perle cotton band in progress is the pattern referred to in the row-by-row instructions for the pattern heddle. The bookmarks show other patterns woven on the same warp.

a few rows in plain weave to establish a good width. The band will narrow a little when the pick-up pattern begins, because the fabric structure is less dense where pattern ends are floating. Be consistent in the direction you start the shuttle (down shed always right to left, for example).

Reading the pattern chart

The chart for the chevron pattern used in the following row-by-row instructions is shown in Fig. 117. Charts are read from bottom to top, in the same direction the weaving proceeds. One vertical column represents one pattern end. One horizontal row of squares represents one row of weft. Charts are drawn on a square grid, but patterns usually appear more elongated when woven.

One repeat of the pattern is marked in red. A dark square means the pattern end is visible on the front on that row, so in making your pattern selection you would take the shuttle under that end. A light square means the pattern end is not visible on the front on that row, so you would take the shuttle over that end. To weave the first row of this repeat you would take the shuttle over 2, under 1, over 3, under 1, over 2. Several rows of plain weave are shown at the beginning and we'll start with those.

Weaving plain weave

For the first row of plain weave make the appropriate shed (the up-shed for most pattern heddles). While holding the pattern heddle in position with the hand opposite the shuttle, select the odd-numbered patterns ends (1, 3, 5, 7, and 9) by taking the point of the shuttle under them, near the heddle where the ends are evenly spaced. With light background ends you can easily see through the ends in the upper level of the shed to select the pattern ends you need.

For the second row select the even-numbered pattern ends (2, 4, 6, and 8). Weave several more rows of plain weave, ending with a row of plain weave that selects the odd-numbered pattern ends. Then weave the next row by not selecting any pattern ends, as shown in Fig. 117. This separates the plain weave from the pattern with a solid line of background color.

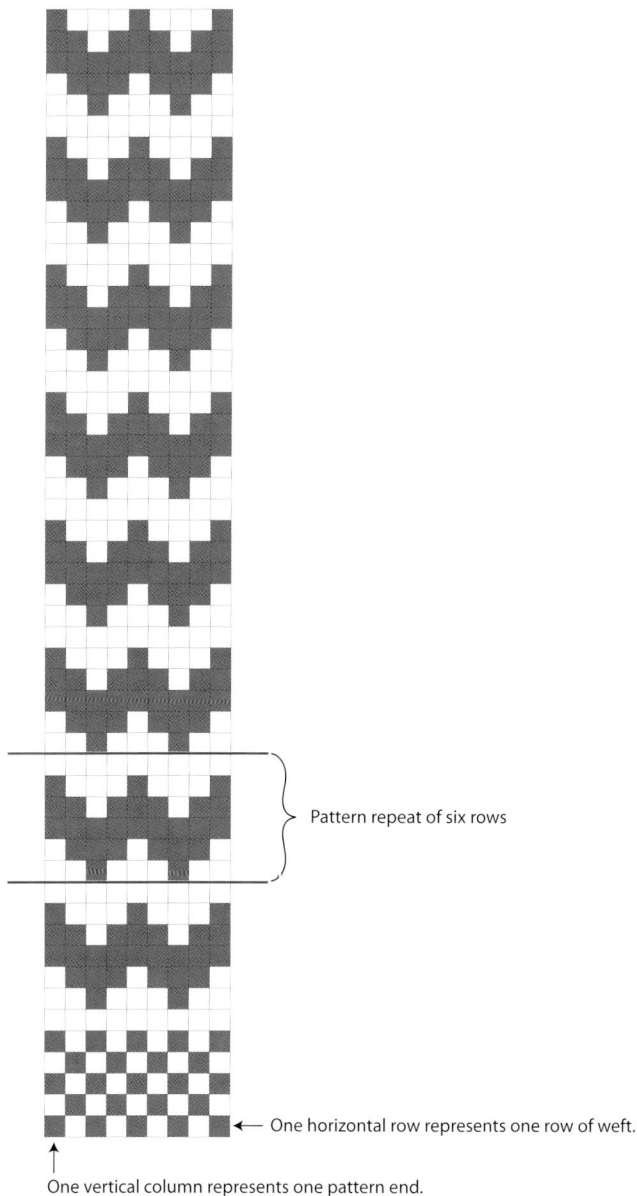

Pattern repeat of six rows

← One horizontal row represents one row of weft.

One vertical column represents one pattern end.

Fig. 117: Chart for band in Type 2 pick-up on the pattern heddle.

Fig. 118: Making a selection on the pattern heddle. I'm weaving the down-shed from right to left. The red pattern ends float in the middle of the shed. With the point of the shuttle I've selected 2, skipped 1, selected 3, skipped 1, selected 2 for this particular row of pattern.

A different rhythm

If you've already woven on a band heddle, you'll notice that there is a different rhythm to weaving on the pattern heddle. Instead of beating the previous row and then making the selection, you'll make the selection and then beat the previous row. The steps are: change sheds, make the pattern selection with the tip of the shuttle, then before you take the shuttle through pull it towards you to beat, and adjust the weft at the selvedge as you take the shuttle through.

Row-by-row instructions

To weave the pick-up pattern, follow the same steps as for plain weave, choosing which pattern ends to select by looking at the chart. Isolate one row on the chart at a time and take the shuttle under the pattern ends represented by dark squares. After you have correctly inserted the shuttle in the shed, the pattern ends in the upper level of the shed will match the corresponding row on the chart.

Row 1: Select Pattern Ends 3 and 7 (the third pattern end from each side)

Row 2: Select Pattern Ends 2, 3, 4 and 6, 7, 8 (two groups of three threads centered above the ends you selected in Row 1).

Row 3: Select all pattern ends.

Row 4: Select Pattern Ends 1, 2, 4, 5, 6, 8, and 9 (all pattern ends except 3 and 7, the ends you selected on Row 1). This row is the exact opposite of Row 1.

Row 5: Select Pattern Ends 1, 5, and 9 (the two edge ends and the middle end). This row is the exact opposite of Row 2.

Row 6: Do not select any pattern ends (take the shuttle over all the pattern ends). This row is the exact opposite of Row 3.

Fig. 118 shows Row 4 being selected. Repeat these 6 rows over and over to form the chevron pattern. Unlike many Type 2 patterns, you'll notice this one looks the same on both front and back.

Determining the correct starting shed

On the pattern heddle, half of the pattern slots are placed in narrow bars and the other pattern slots are placed in wider bars that they share with two holes. If the outermost pattern ends in a particular warp are threaded in narrow bars, you'll use the up-shed to begin if the chart calls for selecting odd-numbered pattern ends on the first row, and the down-shed to begin if the chart calls for selecting even-numbered pattern ends on the first row. If the outermost pattern ends are threaded in wider bars you'll do the opposite.

In most instances you'll use the up-shed to begin with odd-numbered pattern ends, since the pattern heddle is typically constructed with the outermost pattern slots in narrow bars. But if you're weaving a band with 11 pattern ends on a pattern heddle with 13 pattern slots, for example, the outside pattern ends will be in wider bars and the opposite rule will apply.

If all the pattern ends are selected on the first row, to make a horizontal line of pattern color, consider only the ones on the outer edges of the group and ask yourself whether they are odd or even. If a mix of pattern ends is selected in the first row, find a 3-row or 5-row float that begins on the first row. If the float is on an odd-numbered pattern end, start with the shed appropriate for odd-numbered pattern ends.

Weaving more efficiently

I use a different mental approach with the pattern heddle than with the band heddle because the pattern ends present themselves very differently on the two heddles. On the band heddle I'm thinking in terms of how the motif is developing diagonally, while on the pattern heddle I'm thinking in terms of how the motif is built row by row horizontally.

The chevron pattern is so simple that you'll quickly be able to weave it without looking at the chart. You can choose another pattern from the pattern charts for 9 pattern ends in the Pattern Supplement at the end of this **Part**, as I did for the bookmarks shown in Fig. 116. When you weave a motif that

Fig. 119: To rip out a row of pick-up, pull up on the weft as shown and slip your hand into the space occupied by the weft. Then you can take the weft back through.

has more rows in the repeat than the chevron does, try dividing it into smaller sections that are easier to commit to memory. The less you need to look at the chart, the faster you'll be able to weave. Most patterns are symmetrical both horizontally and vertically and are not as complicated as they first appear. The same selections are used over and over, combined in different sequences to create different motifs. In time you'll be able to see these selections as whole units, rather than collections of individual squares, like reading chords in music. You can assign a short code to each selection, like "1s & 5" for selecting one end at each side and five in the middle—something that makes sense to you and allows you to remember a string of three to five selections at a time.

Of course the more pattern ends the band has the more complex this becomes, and in bands with lots of pattern ends you'll want to simply isolate one row on the chart at a time with a ruler. With wider patterns, making selections will be easier if some pattern ends in the warp are a different color—for example if the middle pattern end or the middle three pattern ends are black instead of red to give you a point of reference. It also helps to mark with pencil above the center pattern slot.

You can weave any chart for Type 2 pick-up on the pattern heddle, as long as you have at least as many pattern slots as there are pattern ends in the chart. Disregard any caret and X symbols as you won't use those for the pattern heddle.

Ripping Out a Row

If you notice a mistake and need to rip out a row of pick-up, here's an easy way. Say the row of pick-up you want to rip out was made on the up-shed with the shuttle going from left to right. Make the up shed and with a small tapestry needle, poke into the warp at the left edge to get hold of the weft at the very beginning of the row you want to rip. Push the needle away from you until there is enough slack in the weft to grab onto. Pull up on the weft on both sides of the band, as shown in Fig. 119, and slip your hand into the space occupied by the weft. Then you can take the shuttle back through the modified shed from right to left.

Deciding How to Start a Pattern in Type 2

There are several options for starting the first motif in a Type 2 pick-up band, on either the band heddle or the pattern heddle, as shown in Fig. 120. In the first example, at the bottom of the chart, the first motif is surrounded by plain-weave flecks, so the motif appears to grow out of the plain weave. In the second example, some of the flecks have been omitted to get a clean diagonal line of background color between the plain weave and the motif. In the third example, all the flecks have been omitted on the row before the motif begins, and then the pattern begins in the same way it will be woven in subsequent repeats. In all three examples, the correct placement of the motif in relation to the underlying plain-weave structure has been maintained.

With Knut's Help—A Direct Warping Method

In the 1960s, Aagot Noss visited Oliva Dalen (born 1894) in Hol, Hallingdal, in Buskerud, and documented the techniques Oliva used to weave a narrow hairband in warp-faced plain weave. At that time Oliva still tied up her hair with such hairbands every day, and she wove them on a simple band heddle, made in 1829 and inherited from her great-grandmother.

For warp, Oliva used white cotton and red wool yarn. She used a direct method of warping, measuring the warp between a window hasp and the band heddle, cutting the yarn and threading the band heddle as she went.

First she decided how long her warp would be. Her husband Knut sat in a chair that distance away from the window hasp, holding the band heddle upright in his lap. Her pattern called for ten warp ends of white and ten of red, alternating across the width. She threaded all white ends first and then went back and filled in with red.

To begin, she placed a ball of white yarn in a basket on the floor. She threaded the end through the band heddle with a tapestry needle and gave the end to Knut to hold on the other side. Then she walked to the window with the yarn, looped it around the window hasp and walked back to Knut. There she cut the yarn, threaded the second end of the bout through the band heddle, and then repeated the procedure: thread one end, make a bout, cut, thread the other end. One bout (one round trip from the band heddle to the window hasp and back again) made two warp ends.

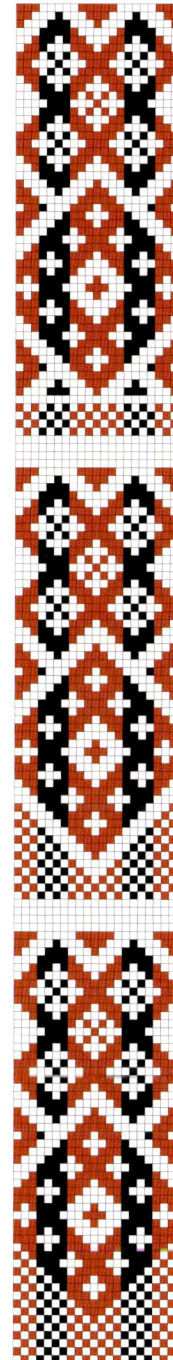

Fig. 120: Three options for starting a Type 2 pick-up pattern in relation to the plain-weave flecks at the beginning. Pattern from man's suspenders from Nordfjord.

Fig. 121: If you have a friend to help hold the warp, you can try this direct warping method.

Oliva began threading in the middle of the band heddle, working out to the sides from there. When all white warp ends were threaded she had five white ends on each side of center. On one side they were threaded through holes and on the other side through slots.

Then she placed a ball of red yarn in the basket and threaded the red warp ends. The colors alternated, so the side that had white ends in the holes had red ends in the slots, and vice versa. Her pattern called for an even number of ends of each color so she had no knots for color changes.

When she was done threading, Knut was holding all the cut ends on his side of the band heddle. To finish the warp she knotted the cut ends together in one big overhand knot, unhooked the other end of the warp from the window hasp, and made a loose crochet chain with the warp length, working towards the band heddle.

To weave, Oliva wound unbleached cotton weft on a wooden netting shuttle. She fastened the warp chain to a window hasp and fastened the other end of the warp to her belt.[5]

A plain-weave hairband like the one Oliva wove was called a *kambeband* (comb band) and was used for everyday wear. Two pick-up patterns used for hairbands in Hallingdal were the chevron pattern, called the *klauveband* (cloven hoof band), and the cross pattern, called the *spåraband* (animals tracks band). The spåraband pattern was used for the finest hairbands, as shown in Fig. 17, **Part 1**.

Pattern Supplement

At the end of this **Part** you'll find charts for dozens of traditional patterns (Figs. 130–150). To explain which warp drafts (Fig. 151) work with these charts, and to illustrate how the patterns might be used in your own projects, several ribbons and other woven items are described below.

Type 1: Kiersti's Coverlet Patterns

The charts in Figs. 130–132 were adapted from bands in Kiersti's coverlet (Fig. 34, **Part 1**), and can be woven on the offset threading shown in Warp Draft 7 in Fig. 151. Kiersti's bands used fifteen pairs of each pattern color in five sections, whereas these charts use nine pairs of each pattern color in three sections for narrower bands. You can see on the warp draft how the light and dark pattern colors change threading position in the center section, and one of the pattern colors also changes in the center section. At the bottom of the charts you can see the offset horizontal bars that appear when the threading is woven in plain weave. The patterns are easy to weave, since most involve simply picking up alternate pairs, either across the width or in certain sections, and the color shift in the center helps you keep your place.

For the journal keeper shown in Fig. 122, I used Maysville Cotton 8/4 in black for the pattern color that stays the same, and Hifa Frid Vevgarn in copper and gold for the pattern color that changes in the center section, for a width of 1". One journal keeper requires a finished woven length of about 24". I left fringe at one end, faced the other end with black wool felt, folded the faced end over two brass rings, and stitched the two layers together on the sewing machine to form a channel for the pen.

Fig. 122: The wool and cotton journal keeper and the two samples to the left use the same warp draft in different colorways and show three of the patterns possible on an offset threading in Type 1.

Fig. 123: These six perle cotton bands could be used as ribbons or bookmarks. They are woven in a variety of colors and show how Type 2 pick-up looks good on either side.

(Opposite Page) Fig. 124: Detail of four of the perle cotton bands shown in Fig 123, back and front.

(Opposite Page) Fig. 125: In this close-up of two of the perle cotton bands shown in Fig 123, you can clearly see the basketweave texture in the background and the embossed appearance of the pattern motifs.

Type 2: 7, 9 or 11 Pattern Ends

The charts for 7 pattern ends in Figs. 133–134 can be woven on Warp Draft 3 or 4, and the charts for 9 pattern ends in Figs. 135–136 can be woven on Warp Draft 6, 8, or 9 (for warp drafts see Fig. 151). For the charts for 11 pattern ends in Figs. 137–138 you can add ends to the narrower warp drafts, following the same arrangement of pattern and background color.

For the bands shown in Fig. 123, I threaded according to Warp Draft 8 or 9 in Fig. 151. I used 5/2 perle cotton in natural white or ecru for background, rust, dark blue, or green for pattern, and various colors for borders, for a width of ⅞". These bands make nice bookmarks, and you can make several on one warp, with a different pattern for each one, allowing for fringe between bookmarks by inserting a piece of lightweight cardboard into a shed.

Fig. 126: The wool and cotton basket band is woven in a pattern from Nord-Østerdalen. The interesting border threading is from Band 1 in **Part 2**.

Type 2: 13 Pattern Ends, Nord-Østerdalen

The patterns in Figs. 139–141 were charted from bands sewn together to make cushion covers in Nord-Østerdalen in the 1800s. They can be woven on any warp draft with 13 pattern ends. The basket band shown in Fig. 126 was woven on Warp Draft 10 in Fig. 151, a threading taken from Barbro Ramseth's bed band (Band 1, **Part 2**). I used Bockens Cotton 8/2 for background, Rauma Prydvevgarn in red and green for pattern, and Hifa Frid Vevgarn in black for borders, for a width of ¾". The border threading yields an interesting braided effect along the edges.

Type 2: 9, 11, or 13 Pattern Ends, Telemark

The charts in Figs. 142–144 are for a variety of Telemark patterns. The belt shown in Fig. 127 was woven using Warp Draft 11 in Fig. 151, which has a main section of 11 pattern ends, and borders in Type 1 pick-up in the Telemark style. Some of the charts have 9 or 13 pattern ends instead of 11, and for these you can omit or add ends to the warp draft as necessary. The Type 1 border pattern is shown only with the chart that I used for this band.

Borders in Telemark bands are often woven with twelve ends (three pairs in each threading position), just like the sample band used for the row-by-row instructions for Type 1 pick-up. Here there are only six ends (three single strands in each threading position), to keep the border from being too wide in relation to the main pattern section in this particular yarn. There are accent stripes in black on either side of the borders. This border threading is from Band 10, **Part 2**.

I used Bockens Cotton 8/2 in natural white for background. The main pattern color is Rauma Prydvevgarn in red, the Type 1 border pattern colors are Rauma Prydvevgarn in red and green and Hifa Frid Vevgarn in gold, and the accent stripe color is Hifa Frid Vevgarn in black. The width is 1". Since black wool is used for edge accent stripes and white cotton is used for weft, this belt has a whipstitched effect on the edges. I faced the ends of the band in black wool felt. One end is folded over two black rings and hand-stitched in place. The facing at this end is 3" long to pad that section of the belt and support the *nøstekrok* (hook for holding ball of knitting yarn).

Fig. 127: The Telemark-style band is made into a belt with double rings for a modern closure. It holds a *nøstekrok* (hook for ball of knitting yarn). A *nøstepinne* (stick for winding ball of knitting yarn) is shown below the belt.

Fig. 128: The pattern in this wool and cotton band is adapted from one in the coverlet on the front of the book, *Årbok for Nord-Østerdalen 1985*.

Type 2: Kiersti's Coverlet Patterns

The charts in Figs. 145–150 are from bands in Kiersti's coverlet (Fig. 34, **Part 1**, also shown on the cover of the book in Fig. 128). Kiersti's bands have two pattern sections, each with 13 pattern ends, separated by a narrow plain-weave stripe. To weave the sample shown in Fig. 128, I omitted the center plain-weave stripe and one of the pattern ends to make a single pattern with 25 pattern ends. I used Warp Draft 12 in Fig. 151, with Bockens Cotton 8/2 for the background, Hifa Frid Vevgarn in copper/rose and gold for the pattern colors, and Hifa Frid Vevgarn in black for the borders, for a width of 1⅛". Unlike the other charts for Type 2 pick-up in this **Part**, the charts in Figs. 145–150 do not show the plain-weave flecks at the beginning of the first motif. You can decide how you want to begin a pattern according to the options shown in Fig. 120.

(Opposite Page) Fig. 129: Detail of wool and cotton band shown in Fig. 128.

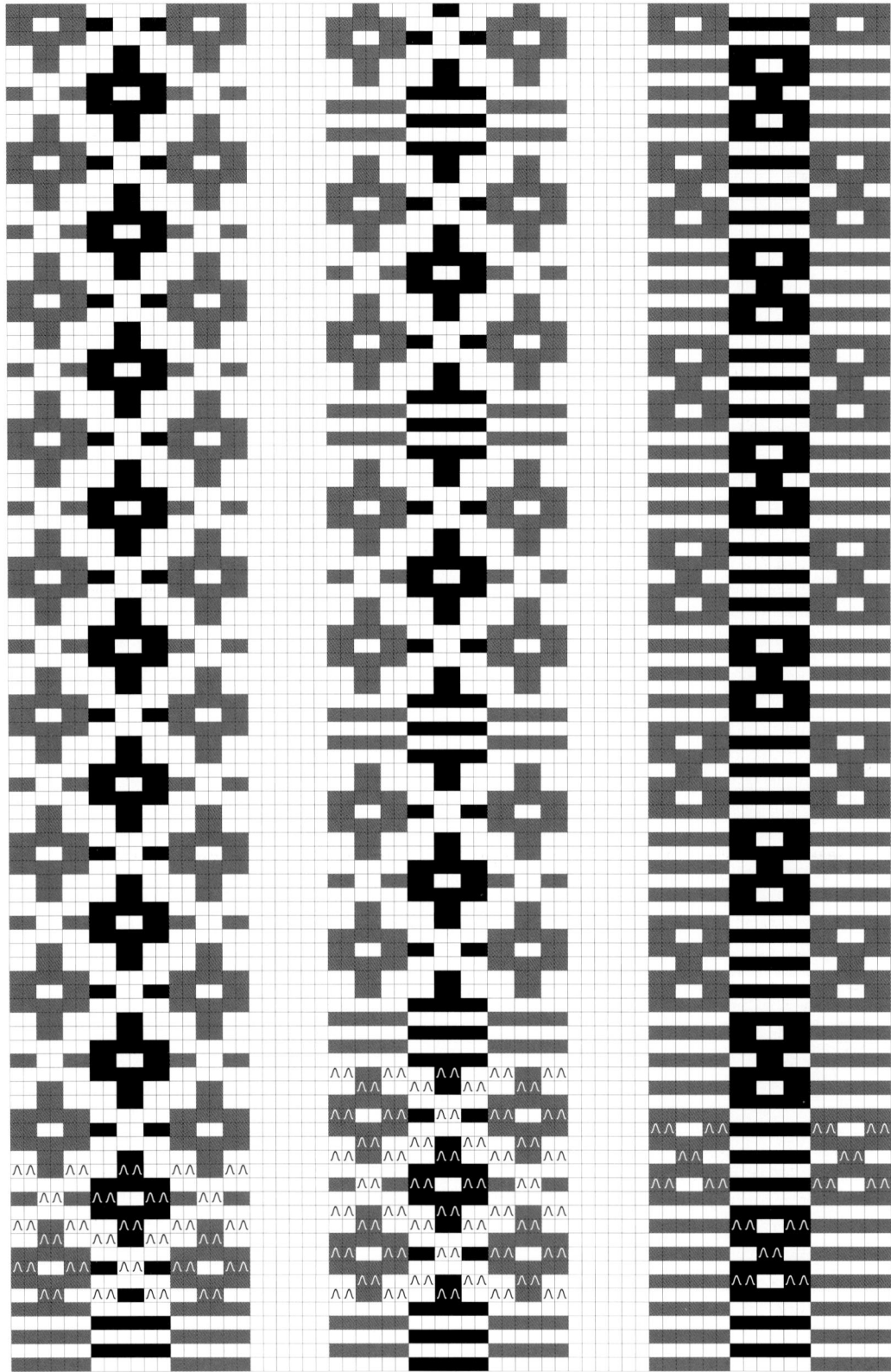

Fig. 130: Charts for Type 1 pickup with 18
pattern ends (9 pattern pairs) of each color.
One of the pattern colors changes to a
different shade in the center section.

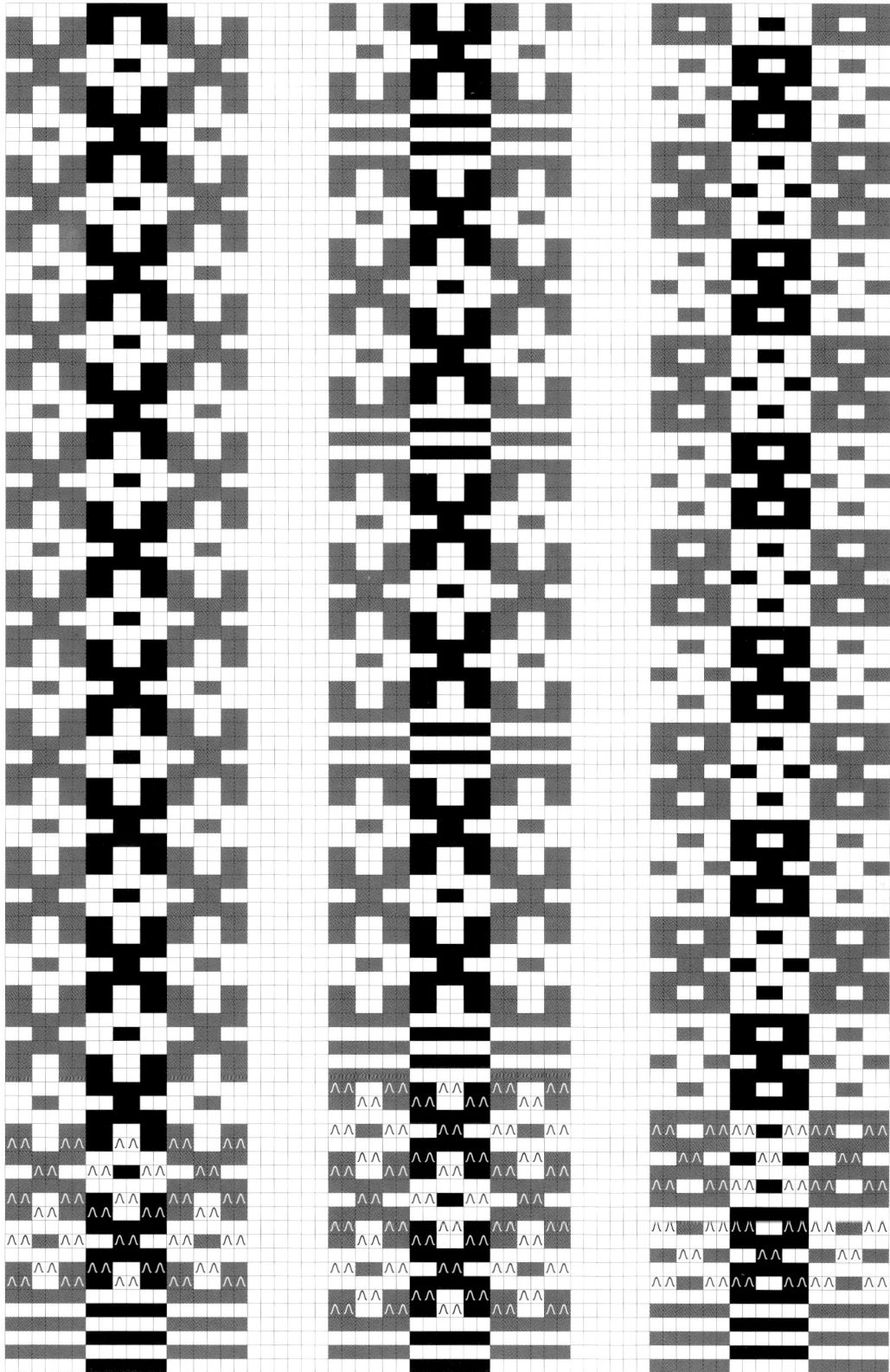

Fig. 131: Charts for Type 1 pickup with 18 pattern ends (9 pattern pairs) of each color. One of the pattern colors changes to a different shade in the center section.

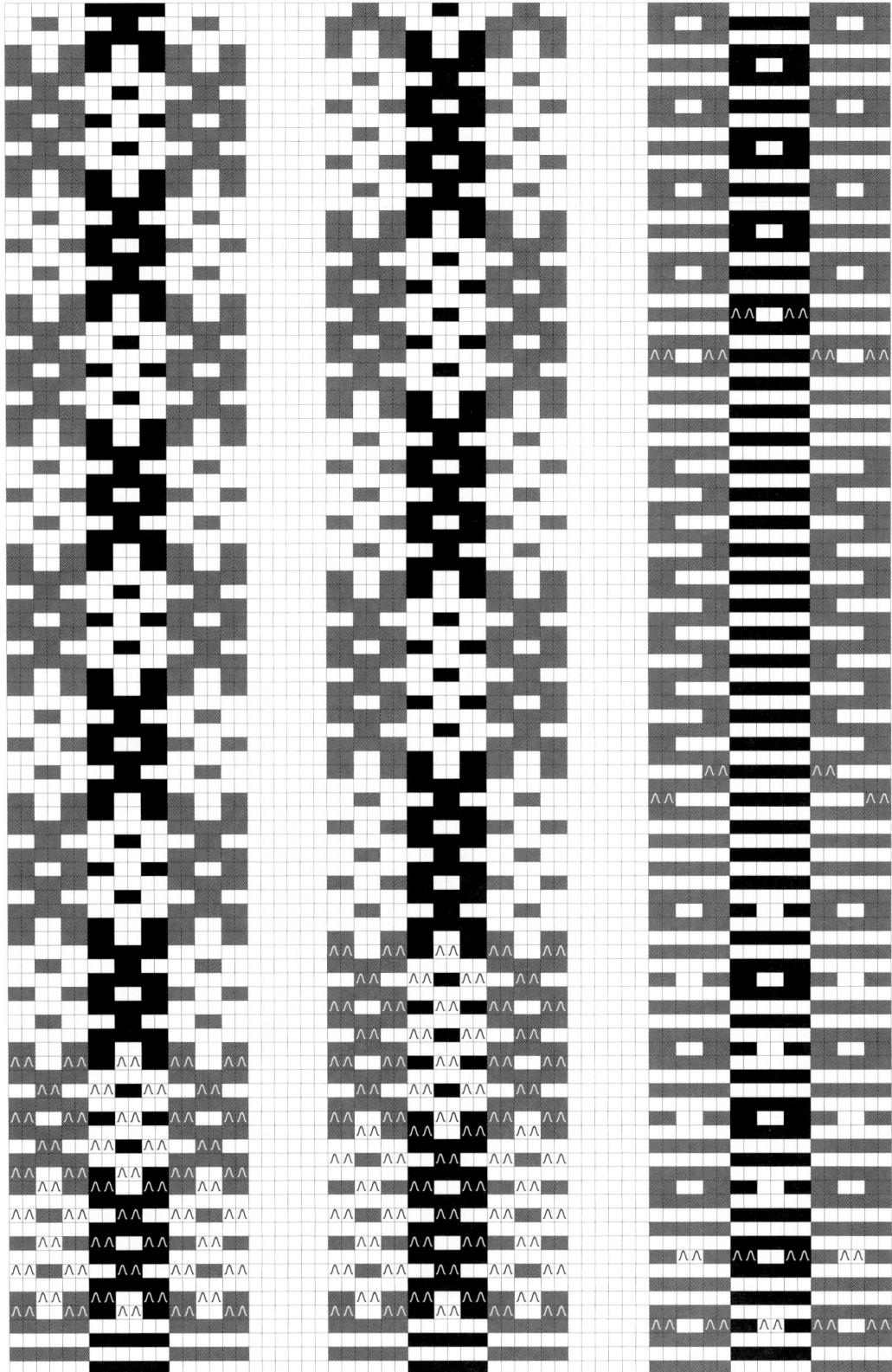

Fig. 132: Charts for Type 1 pickup with 18
pattern ends (9 pattern pairs) of each color.
One of the pattern colors changes to a
different shade in the center section.

Fig. 133: Charts for Type 2 pickup with 7 pattern ends.

151

Fig. 134: Charts for Type 2 pickup with 7
pattern ends.

152

Fig. 135: Charts for Type 2 pickup with 9 pattern ends.

Fig. 136: Charts for Type 2 pickup with 9
pattern ends.

Fig. 137: Charts for Type 2 pickup with 11 pattern ends.

Fig. 138: Charts for Type 2 pickup with 11
pattern ends.

Fig. 139: Charts for Type 2 pickup with 13 pattern ends, from Nord-Østerdalen.

Fig. 140: Charts for Type 2 pickup with 13
pattern ends, from Nord-Østerdalen.

Fig. 141: Charts for Type 2 pickup with 13 pattern ends, from Nord-Østerdalen.

Fig. 142: Charts for Type 2 pickup with 9
pattern ends, from Telemark.

Fig. 143: Charts for Type 2 pickup with 9, 11, and 13 pattern ends, from Telemark. Typical Telemark border shown with third pattern from left.

Fig. 144: Charts for Type 2 pickup with 13
pattern ends, from Telemark.

Fig. 145: Charts for Type 2 pickup with 2
pattern sections, each with 13 pattern
ends, from Nord-Østerdalen.

Fig. 146: Charts for Type 2 pickup with 2
pattern sections, each with 13 pattern
ends, from Nord-Østerdalen.

Fig. 147: Charts for Type 2 pickup with 2 pattern sections, each with 13 pattern ends, from Nord-Østerdalen.

Fig. 148: Charts for Type 2 pickup with 2
pattern sections, each with 13 pattern
ends, from Nord-Østerdalen.

Fig. 149: Charts for Type 2 pickup with 2 pattern sections, each with 13 pattern ends, from Nord-Østerdalen.

Fig. 150: Charts for Type 2 pickup with 2
pattern sections, each with 13 pattern
ends, from Nord-Østerdalen.

Warp Drafts

1  Plain weave in 2 colors

2 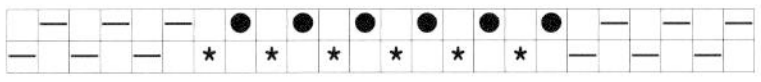 Type 1: 3 pairs of each pattern color

3 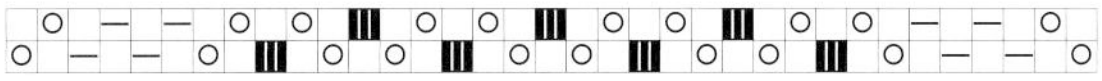 Type 2: 7 pattern ends

4 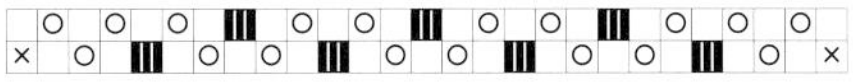 Type 2: 7 pattern ends, whipstitched edge effect

5 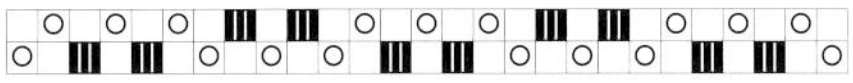 Type 2: Setesdal variation

6 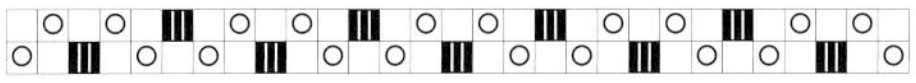 Type 2: 9 pattern ends, no borders

7 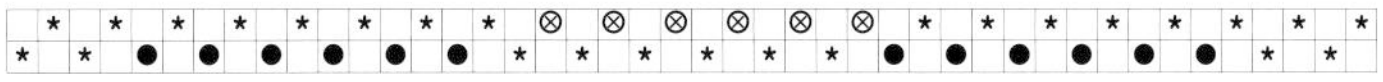 Type 1: offset threading

8 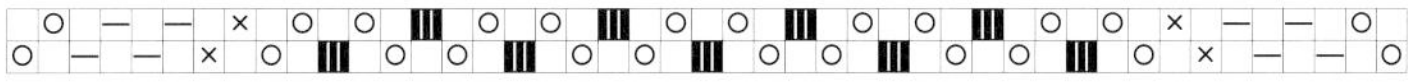 Type 2: 9 pattern ends, striped borders

9 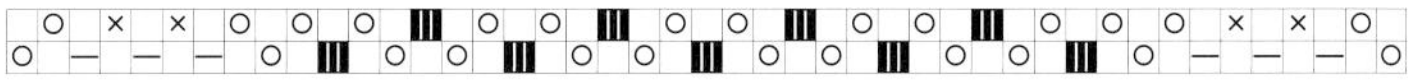 Type 2: 9 pattern ends, barred borders

10 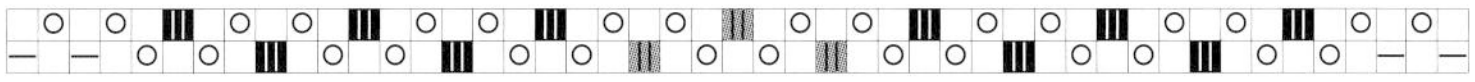 Type 2: Nord-Østerdalen

11 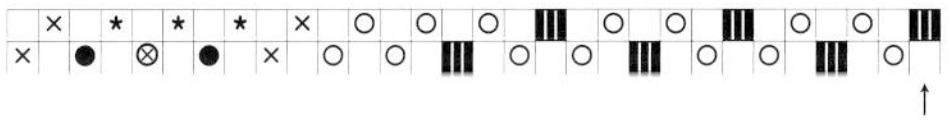 Type 2: Telemark

12 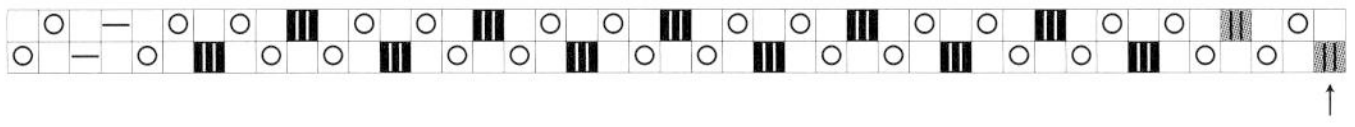 Type 2: 25 pattern ends

Key

— = border color   ↑ = center, when only half of draft shown

× = border color

● = pattern color, Type 1

⊗ = pattern color, Type 1

⋆ = pattern color, Type 1

○ = background color, Type 2

▮ = pattern color, Type 2, twice as thick as background or doubled

Fig. 151: Warp drafts referred to in **Part 3**.

Suppliers

For band heddles and yarn

Glimåkra USA
50 Hall Lane
Clancy, MT 59634
Tel. 866-890-7314
www.glimakrausa.com

Vävstuga Weaving School
16 Water Street
Shelburne Falls, MA 01370-1119
Tel. 413-625-8241
www.vavstuga.com

For band heddles

Vävkompaniet
Västerbrogatan 15
503 30 Borås
Sweden
Tel. 033 - 41 89 99
www.vavkompaniet.se

For Norwegian weaving yarn

Blue Heron Knittery
300 West Water Street
Decorah, IA 52101
Tel. 563-517-1059
www.blueheronknittery.com

Norsk Fjord Fiber
2806 NW 29th Street
Gainesville, FL 32605
Tel. 352-682-3255
www.norskfjordfiber.com

For metal rings

Strapworks
3900 West 1st Avenue
Eugene, OR 97402
Tel. 541-741-0658
www.strapworks.com

For perle and 8/4 cotton

Cotton Clouds
5176 South 14th Avenue
Safford, AZ 85546
Tel. 800-322-7888
www.cottonclouds.com

Halcyon Yarn
12 School Street
Bath, ME 04530
Tel. 800-341-0282
www.halcyonyarn.com

Paradise Fibers
225 West Indiana
Spokane, WA 99205
Tel. 888-320-7746
www.paradisefibers.com

Village Spinning & Weaving Shop
425 Alisal Road
Solvang, CA 93463
Tel. 888-686-1192
www.villagespinweave.com

Webs (mailing address; call for retail location)
6 Industrial Parkway
Easthampton, MA 01027
Tel. 800-367-9327
www.yarn.com

Woolery
315 St. Clair Street
Frankfort, KY 40601
Tel. 800-441-9665
www.woolery.com

Yarn Barn of Kansas
930 Massachusetts Street
Lawrence, KS 66044
Tel. 800-468-0035
www.yarnbarn-ks.com

Endnotes

Introduction and Part 1

1. Jens Erik Jensrud, "Forsidefoto," cover photo.
2. Mary Meigs Atwater, *Byways in Handweaving,* 24, 25, 37.
3. Torbjørg Gauslaa, "Ein tekstilskatt i Nord-Østerdalen," 12.
4. Ibid.
5. Tove Fossnes, "Hælge Beltevever," 30-33.
6. Harald Kolstad, "Friergaver," 7.
7. Janike Sverdrup Ugelstad, "Banke hvitt—mangle glatt," 118.
8. Ibid., 119.
9. Peter Christen Asbjørnsen and Jørgen Moe, "Berthe Tuppenhaugs fortellinger."
10. Aagot Noss, *Frå tradisjonell klesskikk til bunad i Vest-Telemark,* 35.
11. Aagot Noss, *Stakkeklede i Setesdal,* 208, 215.
12. Aagot Noss, *Klesskikk i Tinn i Telemark,* 22.
13. Aagot Noss, *Stakkeklede i Setesdal,* 157.
14. Heidi Fossnes, *Pynting,* 18, 23.
15. Inger Lise Christie, "Dåpslinder fra Østerdalen," 144; *Dåpsdrakter,* 22.
16. Aagot Noss, "Bandlaging," 140.
17. Inger Lise Christie, "Spebarn i «linde og reiv»," 7, 22-26, 30-31; *Dåpsdrakter,* 34-35.
18. Inger Lise Christie, "Spebarn i «linde og reiv»," 26, 42.
19. Ibid., 18, 42.
20. Ibid., 18.
21. Inger Marie Nyeggen and Grete Steigen, eds., *Om daglig liv i Alvdal i nær fortid,* 12.
22. Inger Lise Christie, "Dåpslinder fra Østerdalen," 126; *Dåpsdrakter,* 32.
23. Valle Bygdekvinnelag, *Rette klede i Setesdal: frå vogge til grav,* 14.
24. Inger Lise Christie, "Dåpslinder fra Østerdalen," 126.
25. Inger Lise Christie, "Spebarn i «linde og reiv»," 24.
26. Ingrid Berger, "Dåpsklede i Nordfjord før 1900."
27. Jarle Sanden, "Sendingskorg og sending," 56, 64.
28. Aagot Noss, *Stakkeklede i Setesdal,* 163.
29. Caroline Halvorsen, *Den Norske Husflidsforenings håndbok i vevning,* 7th ed., 179-83.
30. Aagot Noss, *Frå tradisjonell klesskikk til bunad i Vest-Telemark,* 245.
31. Torbjørg Gauslaa, "Ein tekstilskatt i Nord-Østerdalen," 13, 16.
32. Ibid., 7–8.
33. Ibid., 11, 13.
34. Ibid., 9.
35. Ibid.
36. Inger Lise Christie, "Dåpslinder fra Østerdalen," 143, 149.
37. Ibid., 149.
38. Ibid.
39. Anna-Maja Nylén, *Swedish Handcraft,* 196-197.
40. Laurann Gilbertson and Carol Colburn, *Handweaving in the Norwegian Tradition,* 24.

41. Vesterheim Norwegian-American Museum, Berg file, letter to museum May 9, 1984.
42. Laurann Gilbertson and Carol Colburn, *Handweaving in the Norwegian Tradition,* 26.
43. Henry Adams Bellows, trans., *The Poetic Edda,* 207.
44. Norsk Husflid, "Band og bandgrinder," 7; Torbjørg Gauslaa, "Ein tekstilskatt i Nord-Østerdalen," 43–44.
45. Marta Hoffmann, *Fra fiber til tøy,* 183–184.
46. Inger Lise Christie, "Dåpslinder fra Østerdalen," 143; Torbjørg Gauslaa, "Ein tekstilskatt i Nord-Østerdalen," 24; Marta Hoffmann, *Fra fiber til tøy,* 184.
47. Marta Hoffmann, *Fra fiber til tøy,* 185.
48. Ibid., 142, 190.
49. Anastazija Tamošaitienė and Antanas Tamošaitis, *Lithuanian Sashes,* 52.
50. Marta Hoffmann, *Fra fiber til tøy,* 195.
51. Ibid., 197.
52. Ibid., 195.
53. Inger Lise Christie, "Brikkevevde bånd i Norge," 64–65.
54. Torbjørg Gauslaa, "Ein tekstilskatt i Nord-Østerdalen," 21.
55. Ibid., 18, 21, 24.

Part 2

1. Letter from Laurann Gilbertson of Vesterheim Norwegian-American Museum to Author, July 24, 2013.
2. Solveig Zempel, ed., trans., *In Their Own Words,* 102.
3. Ibid, 104.
4. Letter from Helga Reidun Bergebakken Nesset of Nordøsterdalsmuseet to Author, June 20, 2013.
5. Ibid.
6. Ibid.
7. Vesterheim Norwegian-American Museum, Berg file, letter to museum May 9, 1984.
8. Aagot Noss, *Frå tradisjonell klesskikk til bunad i Vest-Telemark,* 35-37.
9. Torbjørg Gauslaa, "Ein tekstilskatt i Nord-Østerdalen," 16.
10. Ibid.

Part 3

1. Helga Reidun Bergebakken Nesset, "Kvite linsvøp og raude band," 55.
2. Aagot Noss, *Frå tradisjonell klesskikk til bunad i Vest-Telemark,* 225.
3. Annemor Sundbø, *Kvardagsstrikk,* 48.
4. Aagot Noss, *Frå tradisjonell klesskikk til bunad i Vest-Telemark,* 224.
5. Aagot Noss, *Bandlaging* (film).

Bibliography

Asbjørnsen, Peter Christen and Jørgen Moe. "Berthe Tuppenhaugs fortellinger." In *Norske Folkeeventyr (1841-1844)*. Linköping, Sweden: Projekt Runeberg, 1996. http://runeberg.org/folkeven/018.html.

Atwater, Mary Meigs. *Byways in Handweaving*. New York: Macmillan Publishing Co., Inc., 1954.

Bellows, Henry Adams, trans. *The Poetic Edda: The Mythological Poems*. Mineola, New York: Dover Publications, Inc., 2004. First published 1923.

Berger, Ingrid. "Dåpsklede i Nordfjord før 1900." Leikanger, Norway: Fylkesarkivet (County Archives) i Sogn og Fjordane, 2007. http://www.fylkesarkiv.no/kl/detalj/?id=104680.

Bergland, Helga Fahre, Ingrid Dillekås Adelsøn, Heidi Fossnes. "De små viktige detaljene." In *Magasinet Bunad,* Nr. 1, 2004. Vollen, Norway: Magasinet Bunad AS, 2004.

Bitustøl, Torbjørg. *Vi vever band med bandgrind*. Oslo: Ernst G. Mortensens Forlag, 1966.

Breivik, Olga Marie, Aud Lysberg, Torun Selstad, Anne-Catherine Sundt, Torild Finsrud Velure, and Vigdis N. Westgaard. *Fanatrøyer*. Bergen, Norway: Eide Forlag, 1998.

Buskerud bondekvinnelag. *Bunader/folkedrakt frå Numedal*. Vikersund, Norway: Caspersens Trykkeri, 1993.

Bunad- og folkedraktrådet. *Norske bunader: bakgrunn, rekonstruksjon, bruk*. Fagernes, Norway: Bunad- og folkedraktrådet, 2003.

Christie, Inger Lise. "Brikkevevde bånd i Norge: levende tradisjon og glemte teknikker." In *By og Bygd: Norsk Folkemuseums årbok, 1983-84*. Vol. XXX. Oslo: Norsk Folkemuseum, 1985.

———. *Dåpsdrakter*. Oslo: C. Huitfeldt Forlag AS, 1990.

———. "Dåpslinder fra Østerdalen." In *By og Bygd: Norsk Folkemuseums årbok, 1979-80*. Vol. XXVIII. Oslo: Norsk Folkemuseum, 1981.

———. "Et reivebarn." In *By og Bygd: Norsk Folkemuseums årbok, 1974-75*. Vol. XXV. Oslo: Johan Grundt Tanum, 1976.

———. "Spebarn i «linde og reiv»." In *By og Bygd: Norsk Folkemuseums årbok, 1981-82*. Vol. XXIX. Oslo: Norsk Folkemuseum, 1983.

———. "Ull og lin: kvinnenes skaperkraft." In *Med egin hand: håndverk og kunst på bygdene*. Oslo: Kaare Berntsen AS, 1993.

Colburn, Carol Huset. "Norwegian Folk Dress in America." In *Norwegian Folk Art: The Migration of a Tradition*. Marion Nelson, ed. New York: Abbeville Press, 1995.

Enerstvedt, Åse. *Vil du vite hvordan de laget og stelte tøy i gamle dager?* Bergen, Norway: Eide Forlag, 1996.

Fossnes, Heidi. *Norges bunader og samiske folkedrakter*. Oslo: J.W. Cappelens Forlag AS, 1993.

———. "Pynting av jente med huvuklut," "Pynting av jente med jentepannelin," and "Pynting av kone med hettebunad." In *Magasinet Bunad,* Nr. 2, 2006. Vollen, Norway: Magasinet Bunad AS, 2006.

———. "Åmlibunaden." In *Magasinet Bunad,* Nr. 3, 2010. Vollen, Norway: Magasinet Bunad AS, 2010.

Fossnes, Tove. "Hælge Beltevever." In *Magasinet Bunad,* Nr. 1, 2004. Vollen, Norway: Magasinet Bunad AS, 2004.

Gauslaa, Torbjørg. "Litt tekstilhistorie frå Nord-Østerdalen." In *Årbok for Nord-Østerdalen 1981*. Tynset, Norway: Musea i Nord-Østerdalen, 1981.

———. "Ein tekstilskatt i Nord-Østerdalen." In *Årbok for Nord-Østerdalen 1985*. Tynset, Norway: Musea i Nord-Østerdalen, 1985.

Gilbertson, Laurann. "To Ward Off Evil: Metal on Norwegian Folk Dress." In *Folk Dress in Europe and Anatolia: Beliefs About Protection and Fertility.* Linda Welters, ed. New York: NYU Press (Berg), 1999.

Gilbertson, Laurann and Carol Colburn. *Handweaving in the Norwegian Tradition.* Decorah, Iowa: Vesterheim Norwegian-American Museum, 1997.

Halvorsen, Caroline. *Den Norske Husflidsforenings håndbok i vevning,* 7th ed. Oslo: J. W. Cappelens Forlag, 1941.

Halvorsen, Kari-Bjørg Vold. "Livet på bygdene," and "Livets høgtider: symbol og gjenstandar." In *Med egin hand: håndverk og kunst på bygdene.* Oslo: Kaare Berntsen AS, 1993.

Hoffmann, Marta. *Fra fiber til tøy: tekstilredskaper og bruken av dem i norsk tradisjon.* Norway: Landbruksforlaget AS, 1991.

HV Konsulentkursen. *Band på många sätt.* Västerås, Sweden: ICA Bokförlag, 1978.

Jensrud, Jens Erik. "Forsidefoto." In *Årbok for Nord-Østerdalen 1996.* Tynset, Norway: Musea i Nord-Østerdalen, 1996.

Kolstad, Harald. "Friergaver." In *Idéhefte for grindvev,* Kirsten Rømcke, ed. Oslo: Norges Husflidslag, 1997.

Koskimies-Envall, Marianne, Jaakko Linkamo, and Erkki Salminen. *The Karl Hedman Art Collection: and selected choices from other collections in the Ostrobothnian Museum,* Vaasa, Finland, 2009.

Larson, Katherine. *The Woven Coverlets of Norway.* Seattle: University of Washington Press, 2001.

Mohr, Vibeke A. *Vår husflid.* Oslo: C. Huitfeldt Forlag AS, 1986.

Nelson, Marion, ed. *Norwegian Folk Art: The Migration of a Tradition.* New York: Abbeville Press, 1995.

Nesset, Helga Reidun Bergebakken. "Bånklæe før i ti'n." In *Årbok for Nord-Østerdalen 2007.* Tynset, Norway: Musea i Nord-Østerdalen, 2007.

———. "Hestan kjem! Om fórbondsreiser til Rørosmartnan." In *Magasinet Bunad,* Nr. 2, 2007. Vollen, Norway: Magasinet Bunad AS, 2007.

———. "Kvite linsvøp og raude band—den eldre dåpskleda i Nord-Østerdalen." In *Magasinet Bunad*, Nr. 3, 2009. Vollen, Norway: Magasinet Bunad AS, 2009.

Norsk Husflid magazine. "Band og bandgrinder." In Nr. 1, 1980. Oslo: Norges Husflidslag, 1980.

———. "Håret." In Nr. 2, 1996. Oslo: Norges Husflidslag, 1996.

Noss, Aagot. "Bandlaging." In *By og Bygd, Norsk Folkemuseums årbok, 1966.* Vol. XIX. Oslo: Johan Grundt Tanum, 1966.

———. *Bandlaging.* Oslo: Statens Filmsentral in cooperation with Norsk Folkemuseum, 1962. Short film.

———. *Frå tradisjonell klesskikk til bunad i Vest-Telemark.* Oslo: Novus Forlag, 2003.

———. *Klesskikk i Tinn i Telemark.* Oslo: Novus Forlag, 1999.

———. *Nærbilete av ein draktskikk: frå dåsakleda til bunad.* Oslo: Universitetsforlaget AS, 1992.

———. "Rural Norwegian Dress and its Symbolic Functions." In *Norwegian Folk Art: The Migration of a Tradition.* Marion Nelson, ed. New York: Abbeville Press, 1995.

———. *Stakkeklede i Setesdal: Byklaren og valldølen.* Oslo: Novus Forlag, 2008.

Nyeggen, Inger Marie and Grete Steigen, eds. *Om daglig liv i Alvdal i nær fortid,* 2nd ed. Alvdal, Norway: Alvdal Bondekvinnelag, 2001.

Nylén, Anna-Maja. *Swedish Handcraft.* New York: Van Nostrand Reinhold Company, 1977.

Pedersen, Kari-Anne. *Bunad og folkedrakt: beltestakk før og nå.* Oslo: Teknologisk Forlag AS, 1997.

Pedersen, Ragnar. "Ting og mening: om å tolke gjenstandene." In *Med egin hand: håndverk og kunst på bygdene.* Oslo: Kaare Berntsen AS, 1993.

Rømcke, Kirsten, ed. *Idéhefte for grindvev,* Oslo: Norges Husflidslag, 1997.

———. *Idéhefte for snorer & band.* Oslo: Norges Husflidslag, 1998.

Sanden, Jarle. "Sendingskorg og sending: Et eksempel fra et belag i Måndalen, Romsdal." In *Dugnad: Tidsskrift for Etnologi 2-1976.* Oslo, 1976.

Simpanen, Marjo-Riitta and Seija Parviainen. *Juho Rissanen: Stained-glass windows.* Helsinki: Bank of Finland, brochure, 2010.

Stokker, Kathleen. *Remedies and Rituals: Folk Medicine in Norway and the New Land.* St. Paul: Minnesota Historical Society Press, 2007.

Stuksrud, Anne Grete. "Band med plukkmønster." In *Årbok for Nord-Østerdalen 1985.* Tynset, Norway: Musea i Nord-Østerdalen, 1985.

Sundbø, Annemor. *Kvardagsstrikk.* Kristiansand: Torridal Tweed, 1998.

Svensøy, Kari Grethe. *"Det va inkje hobby; det va arbeid." Tekstilarbeid i Bykle ca. 1900-1935.* Oslo: University of Oslo, 1987.

Tamošaitienė, Anastazija and Antanas Tamošaitis. *Lithuanian Sashes.* Toronto: Lithuanian Folk Art Institute, 1983.

Thorman, Elisabeth. *Väfnad och bandväfnad i Leksand.* Originally published 1914-15. Reprinted in *Leksands Hemslöjd: 100 år av skaparglädje och gott hantverk.* Sune Björklöf, ed. Leksand, Sweden: Leksands Hemslöjdsvänner, 2004.

Torgenrud, Heather. "Pick Up a Band of Chevrons." *Handwoven,* Jan./Feb., 1996, Vol. XVII, No. 1. Loveland, CO: Interweave Press, 1996.

Trotzig, Liv and Astrid Axelsson. *Band.* Västerås, Sweden: ICA-förlaget, 1972.

Ugelstad, Janike Sverdrup. "Banke hvitt—mangle glatt." In *By og Bygd, Norsk Folkemuseums årbok, 1985 86.* Vol XXXI. Oslo: Norsk Folkemuseum, 1987.

Valle Bygdekvinnelag. *Rette klede i Setesdal: frå vogge til grav.* Norway: Valle Bygdekvinnelag, 1999.

Zempel, Solveig, ed., trans. *In Their Own Words: Letters from Norwegian Immigrants.* Minneapolis: University of Minnesota Press, 1991.

Glossary

Norwegian Words

bandgrind (plural *bandgrinder*, can also be spelled *båndgrind/båndgrinder*) band heddle, hole-and-slot heddle used for bandweaving

bunad (plural *bunader*) modern Norwegian festive costume, based on traditional church-going folk costumes from a specific region and time period

husflid folk crafts or home crafts

All other Norwegian words in the text are translated to English as they appear and thereafter the translation is used, so they are not included in this glossary. Readers who look closely at the Norwegian words will notice that while most Norwegian nouns add *–er* in the plural, some do not. Compound nouns ending in *–band* are the same in singular and plural form, so the Norwegian word for hairbands, for example, is *hårband* (not *hårbander*). About a dozen short quotes in Norwegian are included in **Part 1**, with translations. Since there are many dialects and spelling variations in Norwegian, the same word sometimes appears in different forms from quote to quote. The spelling of the original source is used. All translations of Norwegian quotes by Author.

Weaving Terms

Weaving terms are defined on pages 46 and 98-102.